Have you ever known that you were destined to do something great for God and perhaps even knew what it is you were to do—but didn't know how to get started? Have you ever questioned God as to why He called you and not some other brilliant, talented, flawless person? Have you ever really wanted to participate in Kingdom building, but felt useless, empty, and unqualified? Then *It's Your Call* is a must read for you! Pastor Lawrence Powell combines biblical principles with personal anecdotes to propel one into their destiny. He has a way of "comforting the confronted," but yet "confronting the comfortable." His personal and professional journey the past twenty years is actually a life course. And the principles he has developed, he so willingly shares to help others get started, get finished, and to know that they can finish well. It's an amazing book for amazing people that have an amazing assignment!

—Dr. Wanda Davis Turner
Wanda Davis Turner Ministries, Atlanta, GA

"It's Your Call" will inspire and empower you to grab hold of your destiny and never let go. There are a plethora of principles in this book, but the read is refreshing and straight-forward. Lawrence Powell is undoubtedly a visionary leader with a powerful message, but his voice is distinct and will be one that the nation will strain to hear more of in the next season.

—Teresa Hairston
Publisher, Gospel Today Magazine

IT'S YOUR CALL

7 SURE WAYS TO FULFILL YOUR LIFE'S PURPOSE

LAWRENCE RAPHAEL POWELL

It's Your Call
7 Sure Ways to Fulfill Your Life's Purpose
ISBN 0-88144-291-7
Copyright © 2008 by Lawrence Powell Ministries
PO Box 1623
Rahway, New Jersey 07065

Published by
Victory Publishing
a division of Victory Graphics and Media
9731 East 54th Street
Tulsa, OK 74146
www.victorygraphicsandmedia.com

DEDICATION

I dedicate this book to my lovely wife, Vanessa, for all that you do in helping me fulfill the call of God on my life. The past twenty years have been an amazing journey indeed. I expect the best is yet to come.

Also to my children, Adria, Aaron and Ashlyn. I love you far beyond your most vivid imagination. It is my prayer that each of you will walk with the Lord faithfully all the days of your lives in constant pursuit of Him. Remember diligence pays off (Hebrews 11:6).

To my parents, Hark and Rebecca Powell, for the major role you have played in raising me. I am forever grateful to you for all you have done.

To my sister, Annette, your encouragement through the years has been invaluable. Although you are usually quiet, I have always heard you loudly and clearly. Who would ever believe as children we fought like cats and dogs?

ACKNOWLEDGEMENTS

I am thankful to Jesus Christ for saving me and selecting me for such a high calling. I am humbled and honored to serve in the Kingdom. Not a moment goes by that I am not keenly aware of my dependence on Him. Indeed, it is in Christ that I live, move and have my being.

Thanks to my Agape family. Your constant support has been a vital factor in every success I have enjoyed since being your pastor. Without a vision people perish. Without people visions perish too. Every time I think of you, I thank my God (Philippians 1:3).

Furthermore, thanks to my Executive, Administrative, and Leadership staff for all the work you do behind the scenes in helping effectuate the vision God has called us to fulfill. I sincerely appreciate your commitment to the ministry of excellence and the service you render to the Lord and His people.

Finally, to every one who has ever prayed for me, encouraged me and even corrected me when necessary—thanks a zillion! Keep it coming. I'm just getting started.

FOREWORD

I once read a quote that said "It's Choice-not Chance-that determines your destiny." I agree wholeheartedly with that statement and because you have this book in your hands, I applaud you for making a great choice. Pastor Lawrence Powell is truly a giant in the Kingdom of God and in his new book, *It's Your Call*, he has laid out principles that if applied, will change your life and propel you closer to your calling. Please do not take that lightly.

Unfortunately, many of us have allowed circumstances to cause us to be callous to the truth of God and therefore we miss out on the blessings of God. In order to receive the blessings from Him, we must please Him. The Bible tells us that the way we please Him is by our faith (Hebrews 11:6). We have to believe, and that means believing His Word. So, when I say that the message shared in *It's Your Call* is a tool that God wants to use to connect you to His will for your life, it is up to you to choose to believe.

Don't get me wrong...I know what it is to be discouraged, despondent, and even disappointed with clever church slogans, empty promises of deliverance in three days (if you just sow one thousand dollars), and even the personal pain of frustration when you keep messing up and just can't seem to get it right. But, regardless of what has happened in the past, regardless of your fear of failure, regardless of who has told you that this "God-thing" is not real, I encourage you to make a decision today to Believe!

Let me ask you a few questions. Aren't you sick of being sick and tired? Haven't you had enough of singing those "whoa is me...life is so hard" songs? Don't you want to get at least a glimpse of the abundant life that Jesus' promised you? If you answered "yes" to all three questions, what are you going to do about it? It's time out for lazy saints. God is saying that if you want to grab hold of your destiny, if you want to fulfill your life purpose, if you want to be an ambassador for Him, you can no longer sit idly by and wait for something to happen. God is looking for warriors who, like Jacob, won't let go until He blesses them (Gen. 32:24-26).

Pastor Powell tells us that "pursuit is the proof of desire." You can't be lackadaisical about seeking your destiny and the blessings of God. Now, let's get this straight. If you think the blessings equate to a house, a car, or a twelve foot yacht, you can go ahead and close this book and do it your way. Yes, monetary prosperity may come for you, but having your health, peace of mind, joy, and Holy Ghost power are such greater gifts. Walking in your calling, as Pastor Powell teaches, causes you to be fulfilled and transformed unlike any other experience.

Although it may seem difficult, understanding what you were specifically created to do is not impossible. Why would God create you for a unique purpose yet not tell you what it is? What has happened is that we have not put ourselves in a position to hear clearly from the Lord. We've allowed our Spirit (where the Lord speaks to us) to be distracted, thus we cannot discern the will of the Lord for our lives. Once we make up our minds to be serious about seeking Him and we sincerely ask the Lord for what we want (clarity of your destiny), He will give it to us.

The Message Translation for Matthew 7:11 says it best: *"Don't bargain with God. Be direct. Ask for what you need. This isn't a cat-and-mouse, hide-and-seek game we're in. If your child asks for bread, do you trick him with sawdust? If he asks for fish, do you scare him with a live snake on his plate? As bad as you are, you wouldn't think of such a thing. You're at least decent to your own children. So don't you think the God who conceived you in love will be even better?"*

That's such good news straight out of the Good Book! We have no more excuses. If we simply ask God directly for what we want, as long as it is in His will (John 14:13) we will receive. Take a moment right now to ask God to use the message He has given Pastor Powell in *It's Your Call* to help you learn what your destiny is in Him. Go ahead...we'll wait on you. Are you done? Good, let's move on.

It is important to point out, as Pastor Powell does early on, *It's Your Call* (as with any other material) cannot and should not be used to replace the Bible and your own personal study of the Word. In addition, it is foolish to think that reading *It's Your Call* will protect you from hardships and trials. Recognizing God's plan for your life is not a promise of a pain-free life. Remember you are a warrior. Warrior's are trained and equipped for battle. You cannot be afraid of facing tough times and as a matter of fact, because you know you have the victory, you can look forward to the fight. However, this book can be used as a supplement to help you understand more clearly the principles of the Word.

I am sure that like me, Pastor Powell receives numerous requests from people asking him to be a personal mentor. Because of our calling, we truly have the heart of a shepherd and at times we want to walk personally with each person and help guide them as the Lord directs. However, it is humanly impossible and would be quite arrogant for us to try to be all things to all people. But what we can do is just what Pastor Powell has done in this timely and impactful manuscript...we can share what God has given us in a book format that is accessible to everyone. I have learned that there are different degrees of mentorship or discipling and it does not always have to come through personal relationship. There are many men and women in the Body of Christ who have mentored me in a specific area and they have no idea. I read their books or listened to their tapes and the Lord used them to help me walk through a particular time in my life. I encourage you to allow *It's Your Call* to do the same for you.

We've all heard the popular adage that says 'what you put in is what you'll get out'. Let me apply that to the book you have in your hands. If you choose to read this book, admit that it had some good information and then go on about your life, you will more than likely stay in the same place you were when you started it. I've had people tell me "Bishop, that was a good Word you preached on Sunday," but then on Monday I see them acting the same way. Was it the Word that God gave me that was ineffective or was it their lack of application? I believe it was the latter. If you want to change, don't treat *It's Your Call* like every other book you've read.

Let me give you a few suggestions for taking full advantage of the opportunity that lies ahead of you. Let's embark on a thirty-day challenge. First, find a friend (an accountability partner) that you can trust that will be willing to go on this journey with you. For the next thirty days, set aside time to specifically seek God for His will in your life. Find a quiet place (preferably the same place each day) and take with you your Bible, a notebook, a pen, and *It's Your Call.*

Each day start your time with the Lord by repenting of any sin that would hinder you from entering His presence. Then, after your time of repentance, simply be quiet. Allow your spirit to connect with Him. Continue your time with the Lord by meditating on any scripture that you feel led to study. Then, begin reading a portion of *It's Your Call.* Ask God to illuminate anything that He wants to specifically speak to you. Use the notebook to jot down anything that leaps out to you or write down any directions or mandates that the Lord speaks. Finally, set a time to meet with your accountability partner. The two of you should share what you have learned and encourage one another to be obedient to what you have heard from the Lord. Stay with this process for thirty days and I truly believe God will reveal Himself to you and you will receive greater clarity for your journey.

Pastor Lawrence Powell is a man of God that has been tried in the fire. He has lived through what He is presenting to you in this book. *It's Your Call* is saturated with wisdom presented in a way that is easy to understand. His humor and transparency is refreshing and truly gives you the sense that he is talking directly to you.

Remember, pursuing God is not for the weak at heart. You must be steadfast and determined to lay hold of that which has laid hold of you. Don't give up...keep pursuing, keep pushing and keep praying. *It's Your Call*...Walk in it!

—Bishop Eddie Long

CONTENTS

INTRODUCTION

God has a remarkable plan for your life—no matter who you are or where you came from. God designed your gifts and talents to be used in the earth. If someone had shared with me the lessons that I will share with you in these pages, it would have saved me many difficult days and restless nights, spent doubting my calling and purpose. After seventeen years in ministry, countless trials and triumphs, I now see that the hand of God was on my life from the very beginning. I want to save you some precious time and give you the same assurance I have today that God has an awesome plan for your life.

I know it is not by accident that you are reading this book. I do not believe in coincidences or serendipitous moments. I do believe, however, in Divine appointments, God encounters, and heavenly assignments. That is precisely what this is. In this book, I will share valuable and useful information, designed to help you discover your life's purpose—not with hype, not with possibility thinking, not with quick fixes and tactics; but with sound principles, rooted in God's Word.

You are about to go on a fascinating journey. You will begin to see and understand how your experiences have been preparing you for your purpose all along. Now, let me warn you. This path is not an easy one. It is not for the faint of heart. You cannot be indifferent and indecisive; unmotivated and undisciplined; fearful and fickle. You must focus on discovering and fulfilling your life's purpose and you will find the rewards are greater than you can imagine!

After you read this book, you will never again have to question your significance, or whether God wants to use you. The principles contained herein, will serve as your compass to help guide you along the path your Heavenly Father has laid out for you. Hear His voice.

He is speaking to you today, because He wants to pull you up out of the doldrums of despair, into a place called destiny. Are you ready to go? It's your call. You must decide to pursue your purpose.

You have no doubt been hearing the voice of God or feeling the unction in your heart to do greater things for the Kingdom. This book will help you discover: the next steps to take, what to expect on the journey, what obstacles you will face, and most importantly, how to overcome by the power of God. Regardless of what Satan has told you about your life, despite where you have been or what you have been through; I want you to make Jeremiah 29:11, the foundation for everything you will read in this book. "For I know the thoughts I think toward you, says the LORD, thoughts of peace and not of evil, to give you a future and a hope" (NKJV).

As you read, let the words rekindle the burning embers of your dreams that have been smoldering under feelings of doubt, defeat, and despair. Let God minister to you through every page the importance of your vision and if the passion for your vision has faded, be encouraged that you will once again feel inspired to follow what He birthed in your spirit years ago.

Before we move forward, keep one thing in mind. This book is not simply to be read, but lived. You must live the principles. Do not just skim through the book. Make a commitment that even if you do not read any other book this year, you will read this one, and read it well. Study, internalize, and apply the practical wisdom found in this book. As a result, your life will be changed, and you will be truly equipped to discover your life's purpose.

Remember, the principles will work, if you work them. Now let's get started.

CHAPTER 1

FACE IT. YOU'RE THE ONE FOR THE JOB!

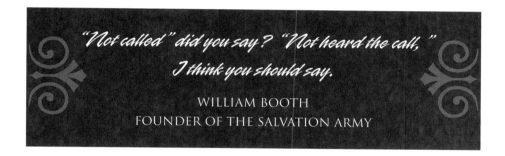

*"Not called" did you say? "Not heard the call,"
I think you should say.*

WILLIAM BOOTH
FOUNDER OF THE SALVATION ARMY

It was a clear sunny day and I could not have been any more than about 5 or 6 years old. I was out in the backyard playing alone in the warm summer breeze. I do not remember why I was alone, but if you ask my mother, she will say that my sister and I used to get into petty squabbles. Our peaceful times of playfulness would somehow decline into: *No! Stop! Move! Get off! Mine! Ouch! Mommy!* And then, we were separated…for safety purposes of course.

This particular day in the backyard was probably no different.

I had an active imagination and I did not really mind playing alone. My "imaginary friends" and I climbed onto my little blue and white, double-seat glider swing set, and I had a captive audience. That day I was performing live in concert, making up one song after another. As I was belting out my original tunes underneath the midday blue sky, I remember hearing myself repeatedly singing these simple lyrics: "Nobody knows me well like the Lord." Now, at the time, I did not realize the profundity of the words. After all, I was just a kid. But somehow, I remember the lyrics so vividly. As I sat there on that swing, I began to sense the presence of the Lord. Everything grew quiet and still, and then, something peculiar happened. The heavens opened up and I heard a voice from heaven saying, "This is my Beloved Son in Whom I am well pleased!" No, no, no…I'm sorry, wrong story. *That* was Jesus.

No, really, I did have an unexplainable encounter with the Lord that day. It was like the old saints used to say, "Somethin' got a hold of me." It reminds me of the Old Testament story of the young prophet Samuel. God called him long before he knew how to distinctly recognize and respond to the voice of God (1 Samuel 3:4-9). Reflecting on that moment in the backyard, I know now with a surety, the Spirit of God was depositing a seed in me, predestined to bloom at a future time.

❧ ENCOUNTERING GOD ❧

I grew up in and around the church, but early on I did not have a clear understanding of God. And I certainly was not aware that I had been divinely selected to touch nations with the message of the Gospel. But by degrees, the Holy Spirit would beckon me more and more, and over the years I came to know His voice better. I wonder, do you remember when you first sensed the majesty, power, and call of God on your life? Where were you? What were you doing? You may not have understood it at the time, and if someone asked you to explain it, you would not have been able to put into words the depth of the encounter.

It is similar to the blind man in the book of St John, who was challenged regarding the healing he received from Jesus. Although he could not explain the experience well enough to satisfy his detractors, his response was simple yet profound. "One thing I know: that though I was blind, now I see" (John 9:25b NKJV). After all these years, I've still not found words to sufficiently express the awesomeness of an authentic God-encounter. But one thing I know, though I was blind, now I see. Take this opportunity to reflect on the moment God began to open your eyes. Remember how you felt? Now softly thank Him for altering the very course of your existence.

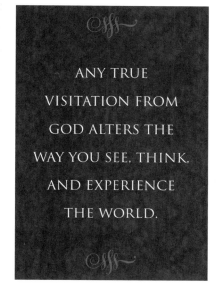

ANY TRUE VISITATION FROM GOD ALTERS THE WAY YOU SEE, THINK, AND EXPERIENCE THE WORLD.

His presence changes you, doesn't it? Of course it does. Any true visitation from God alters the way you see, think, and experience the world. Although the full revelation of His will does not happen immediately, once He deposits His purpose in your heart, you will never be the same again. For me, it was a process that occurred over time. I had to grow, learn, and mature before I could begin fulfilling the call of God on my life. The same is true for you. Don't be discouraged just because you are unable to fully grasp His purpose and plan for your life right now. All you need to know is He has one.

You may not feel that you have a specific calling, and yet, you do. Or, you may not feel like you're qualified, and experienced enough to do what He's chosen you for, but don't worry. He will provide you with everything you need to fulfill your life's purpose.

❧ PERCEIVE THE CALL OF GOD ❧

There is a story found in Mark 8:23–25 about a blind man in Bethsaida, who was brought to Jesus by a group of people. They were begging on his behalf for healing. Jesus took the blind man by the hand and led him out of the town, much the way He leads you and me. He takes us by the hand when we cannot see our way clearly. That's one thing I love about our God. He will never leave you alone, groping in darkness. He will always be there for you.

Jesus began the process of opening this blind man's eyes. The Bible says, "And when He had spit on his eyes and put His hands on him, He asked him if he saw anything. And he looked up and said, 'I see men like trees, walking'" (8:23b–24 NKJV).

It's important to recognize that there was nothing lacking in Jesus' power, only in the man's perspective. The very first time Jesus touched him, he miraculously received his sight. Now, Jesus had to clarify his perspective.

Sometimes, God is dealing with you and showing you things, yet, you don't possess a clear view of His vision for your life. But if you stay in God's presence, He will reveal His will to you. Like this blind man, your vision may be clarified in gradual stages; nevertheless, God will complete the work He has begun in you. Look at what happens in the story. "Then He put His hands on his eyes again, and made him look up. And he was restored and saw everyone clearly" (8:25 NKJV). I speak victory over your life today and declare that, if you can look up with eyes of faith, God will cause you to see what you were not able to see before!

God wants you to recognize His call on your life and begin viewing things from His perspective. Are you ready? Let's continue along the path to perceiving and understanding your calling more clearly.

As you embark upon your own journey, remember to keep your focus fixed on Jesus, the author and finisher of your faith (Hebrews 12:2). Only He can show you who you really are. I'm not saying that there aren't valuable books, trainings, and other resources available to assist you in enhancing your life in some way. In fact, I encourage you to be a life-long learner and seek out practical tools to help you grow and advance. Be aware though; you cannot depend upon self-help books, advice columns, and the well-meaning opinions of close friends and family members, to help you understand and fulfill your Divine calling.

Outside of God, there is no real revelation of truth. His purpose and plan is the only one that will help you live the abundant life He intends for every believer. You may wonder how can you begin truly understanding your purpose and calling. There is a clue found in the book of Ephesians 1:11. The word "purpose" in this passage of Scripture is the Greek word "prothesis," meaning "to lay out beforehand," much like the blueprint of a building. Thus, it conveys the exciting idea that your life has been designed with forethought, predetermination, and deliberate intention. (See also Ephesians 2:19–22.) Isn't that wonderful to know you are no accident? You are not here by happenstance.

The Lord, the Master Architect, has created you with a specific plan in mind. No one else understands the intricacies of your design quite like the One who created the blueprint. This is precisely why positive thinking, dreaming, goal-setting, planning, and networking, without God is grossly overestimated. Remember, "Except the LORD build the house, they labor in vain that build it" (Psalm 127:1a).

❧ TIME IN HIS PRESENCE ❧

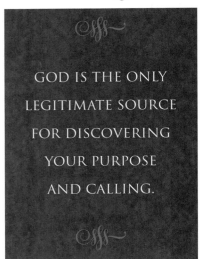

GOD IS THE ONLY LEGITIMATE SOURCE FOR DISCOVERING YOUR PURPOSE AND CALLING.

God is the only legitimate source for discovering your purpose and calling. As you come honestly and humbly before the Father in pursuit of His will for your life, the Spirit will teach you all you need to know. Paul prayed to this end, "that the God of our Lord Jesus Christ, the Father of glory, may give to you the spirit of wisdom and revelation in the knowledge of Him, the eyes of your understanding being enlightened; that you may know the hope of His calling, what are the riches of the glory of His inheritance in the saints" (Ephesians 1:17–18 NKJV). Please understand—the wisdom and revelation for which Paul prayed only comes through time spent in the presence of the Lord.

The more you are in His presence, the more you learn His voice. The more you learn His voice, the more you understand His will. As you grow in your understanding of God's Word, you will begin walking out the steps He has ordered for you before the foundation of the world. You indeed have a set path and it's your job to seek God for direction. This is something I learned early on in my personal pilgrimage. "Counsel in the heart of man is like deep water, But a man of understanding will draw it out" (Proverbs 20:5 NKJV).

Growing up in the church, I remember having a sincere desire to understand the concept of spirituality and what role it played in my life. As I matured, I moved from mere curiosity to genuine interest, and finally, to a deep longing to know God more intimately. Having said that, allow me a moment of transparency. In all honesty, it was the tyranny of my "Dear Mother" that kept me in church every time the doors opened. No, I'm kidding...well, half kidding.

In the Pentecostal church I grew up in, Sunday service was an all day affair. The old saints used to sing a song that said, "Put yo' time in. Pay day is comin' after while." And on Sundays, I think they meant it—literally. I often preferred going to church with my father, because at the particular Baptist church he attended, morning service began at eleven o'clock sharp and it was over at one o'clock on the dot. But don't get me wrong, even though it was only a couple of hours, it felt more like the long, hot summer road trips we took from

New Jersey to Florida each summer for vacation. During these excursions, the only question on my mind was, "Are we there yet?"

If I could have combined the excitement of my mother's Pentecostal church with the abbreviated schedule of Daddy's Baptist church, it would have been a near perfect worship experience!

Although I did not enjoy the excessively extended hours at Mommy's church, I had grown quite accustomed to, and fond of, the energy and exuberance of the Pentecostal style of worship. The distinct rhythmic beating of the tambourine and drums, the syncopated sounds of the Hammond B-3 organ, and the lively demonstrations of praise, were thrilling. But I would soon discover that the thrill was far more than the music.

Little did I know then, you cannot be in the presence of the Lord and not be impacted by the experience. A transformation was taking place in me before my very eyes. God was actually molding me into a vessel of honor to be used by Him, but I did not perceive it at the time. Even as you are reading this book, God is working on you— reshaping your mentality and calling you to a new place in Him. You may not fully understand His plan at the moment, however, just as the aforementioned blind man did, you too must grab hold of His hand. Let Him lead you out of your *Bethsaida* into a new dimension of revelation and clarity.

❧ ACCEPT THE CALL OF GOD ❧

Whenever you branch out and chart a new course along the road God has laid out for you, it is natural to feel some uncertainty. It seems so tough at the time, because you are challenged to do things you have never done before. All kinds of thoughts run through your mind. You wonder if you are really capable of doing what God is challenging you to do. You know you don't want to remain in your current position. At the same time, you feel too afraid to go to an unfamiliar place. You also do not have a single ounce of tangible evidence that God is even speaking to you. How do you get to the point of fully accepting the call of God?

Abraham, who is called the Father of Faith, would probably give you a very concise answer. It would sound something like, "Just do it." How do you think he must have felt when God told him, "Get out of your country, From your family And from your father's house, To a land that I will show you" (Genesis 12:1 NKJV). Sure, Abraham obeyed, but the decision certainly wasn't an easy one. He was being pushed to embark upon a new journey, with most of the details missing. Sound familiar? You see, God knows the end from the beginning. You just have to trust Him. The most important thing is that Abraham obeyed God, accepted the call, and stepped out in faith. God expects no less of you.

You may not have all the particulars. However, God will unfold His plan as you progress along the path He's chosen for you. If you are waiting for Him to perfectly map out the course before you respond to His call, then you'll be left waiting forever. He develops and strengthens your faith as you walk with Him daily. But you have got to start walking.

Whether you are launching a ministry, business, career, product, service or other venture; the same is true of each. You have to start somewhere. Although you may not have all the answers, that cannot be your excuse for doing nothing. You will no doubt make some mistakes; it happens to the best of us. Still, you can't let that stop you.

I remember one day, I got a call from my good friend, Pastor Donnie McClurkin. He is a world renowned Gospel singer, songwriter, and recording artist. On this occasion he was invited as a special guest at a White House Christmas dinner and invited me to tag along! I thought, why not? What an opportunity. I had not visited the Capitol since my ninth grade school trip. Of course, I wanted to make sure I was appropriately dressed. I asked what type of clothing I should wear and Donnie told me it was a black tie affair.

On the day of the event, I made sure I looked the part. I got a fresh hair cut. I put on my black Versace frock coat, custom-tailored shirt and pants. If I had to say so myself, it looked as if I had just fallen off the cover of a *GQ Magazine*. I must admit, I was feeling pretty good about going to the White House that day. When I walked, it was as if I had my own theme music playing in the background. It was *that* serious!

We arrived at the White House, went through the security check, and then, on to the room where the dinner was being held. Quickly, my eyes spanned the room. Then, the record scratched. My theme music abruptly stopped. And I knew…Donnie had not been given the correct information about the evening's dress code. Everywhere I looked, the men were wearing blue and grey business suits.

At that very moment, I knew the answer to the riddle, "What's black and white and red all over?" Me. I felt my face flush. My palms got sweaty. If I could have slid under a table without being noticed, I would have. To say that I was embarrassed, would be putting it mildly. I was utterly mortified. As I stood there in my formal wear, I expected someone to hand me a serving tray at any moment. Clearly, I looked like a resident butler, much like Geoffrey from *The Fresh Prince of Bel-Air*.

In that instant, I had two options. Either I could play "Cinderfella" and storm out of there like it was midnight. Or, I could laugh about it and still choose to enjoy the evening. After I got over the initial shock of it all, I chose the latter. Consequently, I met great leaders from around the country, took pictures with the President and First Lady, and no one seemed too put off by the fancy threads. Despite being overdressed, to my surprise, the evening turned out great. As the lyrics to one of Donnie's hit songs say, "We fall down, but we get up." If you don't always get things right, it is not the end of the world. Just pick yourself up, dust yourself off, and "Keep on truckin'", like Eddie Kendricks used to say.

There may be a few missing details along your path, but don't worry. Things will still work out. Rather than focusing on all you don't know and how out of place you may feel, begin to see the opportunity in front of you. Surely, I could have high-tailed it out of there, but what good would that have done? It really was not that major. At least I can see that now. While it was happening, however, it appeared much more important than it actually was.

Similarly, when you are called to take on a new position, it may seem very intimidating at the time. You may not feel prepared, or qualified. Still, you have been singled out for the job, so you might as well face it. Own it. Trust me, I know it can be difficult to overcome paralyzing fear and the haunting sense of your own inadequacy; accept the job anyway. Ignore that nagging voice whispering in your ear telling you, "God didn't say that. He's not really speaking to you. It's all inside your head." Although you may not feel completely confident, trust God anyway.

Are you familiar with the story of Gideon, the fifth judge of Israel? He was challenged by God to go into battle and defeat the Midianites, on behalf of the nation of Israel (Judges 6:36–38). When Gideon received his assignment, he was ambivalent about the mission. Gideon was not sure that he should be the one leading Israel into battle. After all, of his own admission, he was the least likely choice. He could not imagine why God would hand-pick him for the job.

Gideon was by no means a great warrior and naturally he was confused about why God called him to complete a task that was way out of his league. He was very distraught about the whole thing and could not resist sharing his dilemma with God. Gideon thought that he should probably give God a heads up to help Him understand why choosing him was such a huge mistake.

He said, "O my Lord, how can I save Israel? Indeed my clan *is* the weakest in Manasseh, and I *am* the least in my father's house" (Judges 6:15 NKJV). What did he think God was going to say? "Oh Gideon, you're so right. What was I thinking? I had no idea about your deficiency. Whew! That was a close call." Now, of course, God was not going to agree with Gideon's excuses, just as He's not going to agree with yours. Here is what God actually said, "Surely I will be with you, and you shall defeat the Midianites as one man" (Judges 6:16 NKJV).

Let me help you with something. God is not put off by your (what I call) least-likeliness. It does not matter that you have been considered least likely to succeed, least likely to get the promotion, least likely to survive in business, or least likely to make an impact in ministry. God has called you and He is on your side. It's time to change your attitude and your words. Yes, you are the least likely; that's right. You are the least likely to fail, least likely to quit, and least likely to be defeated. You are *more than a conqueror through Christ Jesus* (Romans 8:37 NKJV).

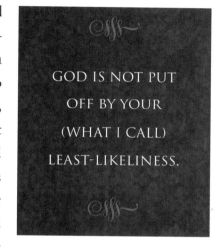

GOD IS NOT PUT OFF BY YOUR (WHAT I CALL) LEAST-LIKELINESS.

It does not matter if you feel unqualified. Being unqualified does not disqualify you from being called by God. He is not deterred by your lack of experience and credentials. God is not limited by your natural limitations and He is in no way restricted by your restrictions. All you have to do is accept His call and He will take care of the rest. As the story continues, we learn that Gideon got cold feet before it was time to go to battle. He asked God to provide some kind of sign to let him know if He had truly called him to embark upon what seemed to be a kamikaze mission.

"So Gideon said to God, 'If You will save Israel by my hand as You have said—look, I shall put a fleece of wool on the threshing floor; if there is dew on the fleece only, and it is dry on all the ground, then I shall know that You will save Israel by my hand, as You have said'" (Judges 6:36–37 NKJV). Verse 38 of that same chapter tells us, that God indeed provided the sign exactly as Gideon requested and everyone was happy, right? No. Not quite.

Actually, verse 39 shows us that Gideon still was not satisfied. He still needed more proof. He asked God for another sign. Essentially, Gideon wanted God to give him a confirmation, for his confirmation. He knew that he was in no way cut out to do what God called him to do.

God did not get frustrated with Gideon; rather, He provided him with another sign to demonstrate that He had indeed called Gideon to do His will. When God calls you, He always puts you in positions you feel woefully inadequate to occupy. Not to worry, because whomever He calls, He equips to do the job—and do it well. Israel went on to win that battle against the Midianites, because Gideon was finally obedient to the call of God.

I'm sure you can relate to the emotions he felt. You may be experiencing a situation in your life where you need God to confirm that He is indeed with you. God has strategically orchestrated this moment to let you know that He is going to complete His work through you. You do not have to fear. He is ushering you into your destiny.

God is speaking to you and He will not be silenced. He is ministering to you right now and He wants you to embrace what He is doing. His call on your life is for specific reason, a distinct purpose, and a set time. God is calling you. Trust me. He will stop at nothing to get your attention.

Think for a moment. Have you been bombarded with confirmations of God's promises? Has He spoken to you in dreams, in visions, or through others? Be sensitive. Be open. Be prepared to fulfill the call. It is time to do what He has instructed you to do.

I know that you, like Gideon, just want to be sure. You want to "know, that you know, that you know" it is truly God. How many times and ways does God have to reveal Himself, before you will say yes to His call? When the voice of the Lord spoke to Isaiah and said, "Whom shall I send, and who will go for Us?" Isaiah told God, "Here am I! Send me" (Isaiah 6:8 NKJV). God wants you to tell Him the same thing, "Here am I! Send me."

When I was coming up in the Church of God In Christ, we would repeatedly say, "Yes Lord," and "Have your way Lord," in times of prayer and worship. That simply meant we were assuming a position of complete submission. We were giving up our own will in exchange for His. If you are going to experience God's best, you must strive to let God have His way in every area of your life. Give Him the opportunity to speak to your heart. Remember the old hymn that says, "Have Thine own way Lord, have Thine own way. Thou art the potter, I am the clay. Mold me and make me, after Thy will. Whilst I am waiting, yielded and still?" (*Have Thine Own Way, Lord,* Adelaide A. Pollard and George C. Stebbins, Hope Publishing 1907,

1935). Let God know that you willing to receive everything He has for you and open to the new dimensions to which He is calling you.

❧ PURSUE THE CALL OF GOD ❧

When I began growing in my understanding of God, I knew that His call was on my life, but I still wrestled and wondered, "Could I really be called? Me, Lawrence Powell? Could God really use me for His glory? Could I be singled out to make a difference in the world?" You may ask some of these same kinds of questions. I want to assure you the answer is yes! God has great plans for your life—much bigger than you can imagine. So big, in fact, they would overwhelm you if He revealed them all at once. You are going to have to passionately pursue the call through intense prayer and supplication.

I recall my earlier days, attending graduate school at Oral Roberts University. I was experiencing a time of tremendous spiritual growth and development in my walk with the Lord. Still, I was seeking to understand exactly how God wanted to use me. One day, while I was in my room alone, I went into my literal prayer closet for a time of deep reflection, introspection, and prayer. That day, I was intent on asking God for direction. I was so full of questions and I really needed to gain a grasp of what He was calling me to do. I began to pour my heart out to Him. I said, "God, whatever You want me to do, I'll do, but I need to know that it's You speaking to me."

I diligently sought the Lord and pushed past my fears, my anxieties, and my concerns. God spoke to me and assured me of His plans for my life. However, this was not the first time, nor would it be the last, that I sought God for His direction and confirmation. You see, I had a constant battle raging in my mind that kept me feeling uneasy, uncertain, and unsure about the path I should take. But I never stopped pursuing His call, even when I didn't understand.

Don't worry just because you don't completely understand everything about your purpose today. You can still apprehend what you cannot comprehend. Simply respond to God as young Samuel did by saying, "Speak, for Your servant hears" (1 Samuel 3:10b NKJV). This kind of act puts you in the right place to receive a word from the Lord.

Pause for a moment now and sincerely ask God to supernaturally develop your ability to discern His voice. Once you recognize His call and become more open to hearing from Him, you will realize that He wants to take you under His wing as His dear child and impart His purpose into your heart. From this day forward, become resolved as never before to pursue your calling intentionally, passionately, and relentlessly.

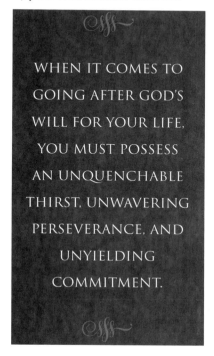

WHEN IT COMES TO GOING AFTER GOD'S WILL FOR YOUR LIFE, YOU MUST POSSESS AN UNQUENCHABLE THIRST, UNWAVERING PERSEVERANCE, AND UNYIELDING COMMITMENT.

When it comes to going after God's will for your life, you must possess an unquenchable thirst, unwavering perseverance, and unyielding commitment. Showing up on Sunday mornings out of habit and mere obligation is not sufficient. Reading a few verses on a bi-monthly basis from your over-sized, large-print family Bible on the living room table won't cut it. An occasional, "Now I lay me down to sleep" prayer is not enough. Quoting, "Jesus wept" (John 11:35), will hardly sustain you during your times of uncertainty.

Pursuit is the proof of desire. Thus, if you approach your quest with a nonchalant attitude, devoid of the true passion it takes to ultimately realize God's plan for your life, you will be met with frustration. Your yearning to understand His calling must infiltrate the very core of your being and cause you to seek Him with true sincerity and fervency in prayer. As you seek God, He will reveal the mysteries of His will in a way that only He can. But you must remain steadfast. You can do it! Just the fact that you are reading this book shows that you have what it takes to overcome adversity, pursue God, and fulfill your destiny.

I cannot tell you how many times I cried out to God from the depths of my being, as I struggled to know exactly what He wanted me to do. I heard His beckoning. I sensed His will. I wanted more clarity, but the answers continually eluded me. I knew God was leading me on a path, but like the proverbial "carrot on a stick," the answers I so desperately craved, seemed to be dangling just beyond my grasp. Yet, I could not quit. Why? The call of God penetrated the very fiber of my being. The passion to pursue His plan became like an unquenchable fire that burned deep inside the recesses of my soul.

God will ignite a burning desire in you to fulfill a higher calling. He will stir up a fire in you to fuel your faith through times of fear and ambiguity. On this journey to discover and fulfill the call of God, you may feel like you are on an emotional rollercoaster, but continue to press on. Remember, when you are serious about seeking God, you are guaranteed to go through periods of uncertainty. Still, don't be deterred. Just keep seeking Him. Hebrews 11:6 says, "...he who comes to God must believe that He is, and He is a rewarder of those who diligently seek Him" (NKJV).

Know that even though things may not come together all at once, God will complete the work He has begun in you. It pays to seek the Lord. Don't give up your search to understand His call. When you seek Him, you will find Him, and when you find *Him*, you will find *you*. Then, the details of your call will be made clear.

These foundational principles are so important. Remember and rehearse what you have learned in this chapter. These principles will assist you in developing your faith during every stage of your journey. Never forget, God has indeed chosen you to complete an assignment that was laid out before the foundation of the world. As you walk with Him, He will continue to unfold His plan.

CHAPTER 2

GET PAST YOUR PAST

Our history is not our destiny.

ALAN COHEN
CONTRIBUTING AUTHOR,
CHICKEN SOUP FOR THE SOUL

A well known speaker started off his seminar by holding up a $50 bill. In the room of 200, he asked, "Who would like this $50 bill?"

Hands started going up and waving excitedly! He said, "I am going to give this $50 to one of you in this room—but first, let me do this." He lowered the bill and proceeded to crumple it between both palms. He then asked, "Who still wants it?" Yet again, the hands went up in the air and the level of excitement escalated even higher.

"Well," he replied, "what if I do this?" He opened his hand and dropped it on the ground, then started to grind the bill into the floor with his shoe. Finally, he picked it up, now crumpled *and* dirty. "Now, who still wants it?" Once more, hands shot up into the air.

He paused and looked at the eager crowd and said, "My friends, you have all learned a very valuable lesson. No matter what I did to the money, you still wanted it, because it did not decrease in value. It was still worth $50. Like this bill, many times in your life, you were dropped. You were crumpled and ground into the dirt, because of some bad decisions, mistakes, and adverse circumstances that came your way.

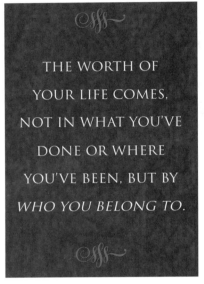

THE WORTH OF YOUR LIFE COMES, NOT IN WHAT YOU'VE DONE OR WHERE YOU'VE BEEN, BUT BY *WHO YOU BELONG TO.*

You feel as though you are worthless, like you've messed up too bad to be valued. But no matter what happened or what will happen, you will never lose your value. Dirty or clean, crumpled or finely creased, you are still, and always will be, priceless to God. The worth of your life comes, not in what you've done or where you've been, but by *Who you belong to.* You are special—don't ever forget it."

You are so amazingly valuable to God. Even if you have experienced divorce, abuse, poverty, abandonment, neglect, or any other unfavorable circumstances, it still does not change the fact that you are chosen by God. He does not want any of your past mistakes holding you back from answering the call He has on your life. You can be delivered from the old wounds and scars that have kept you locked up in the prison of guilt and shame. It's time to get rid of the shackles that have restrained you from breaking free into the destiny that God so desperately wants you to fulfill. He has released you from the sin of your past. Let it go.

At some point, we have all messed up. No one is exempt. The Bible is replete with examples of people who stumbled, but God did not kick them to the curb. In the book of Genesis, Abraham lied and told Pharaoh that his wife Sarah was his sister instead of his wife. He feared that the king would kill him, in order to steal his beautiful bride. Notwithstanding, as I mentioned earlier, Abraham is known as the "Father of Faith"(Genesis 12:11–20).

In the book of Joshua, the woman Rahab was a Canaanite prostitute. Yet, after she protected the Israelite spies from being discovered, apprehended, and killed in the city of Jericho, she found favor with the Lord (Joshua 2:1–15). Scripture reveals that Rahab went on to become part of the lineage of King David, out of which, Jesus Christ, the Messiah came (Matthew 1:5). There are countless other people in the Bible that were flawed. But God, in His infinite mercy, saw fit to use them for His glory. "Oh, give thanks unto the LORD, for He is good! For His mercy endures forever" (Psalm 107:1 NKJV).

God's calling on your life, has nothing to do with your personal worthiness. "For all have sinned and fall short of the glory of God, being justified freely by His grace through the redemption that is in Christ Jesus" (Romans 3:23–24 NKJV). Others may judge you and ruthlessly criticize you, but God is not like man. He loves you, and you are His prized possession, created in His own image (Genesis 1:26).

GET RID OF WEEDS AND POISONOUS SEEDS

It is so easy to fall into the trap of second-guessing your value once you have been exposed to bitter, toxic, and critical influences. Stinking thinking can kill your sense of worth. Don't let this happen to you. Guard your thoughts and bring them into submission to the word of God. You cannot afford to internalize the lies and venomous words Satan tries to plant in your mind. Nothing would bring him more pleasure than for you to let those poisonous seeds take root in you heart, grow, and choke out the call of God on your life.

It's just like I discussed in my previous book, *The Power of the Seed*—whatever you plant and cultivate will grow. Each seed is genetically designed to produce after its own kind (Genesis 1:11). It is a fundamental principle. That is why you must be very careful about what seeds are sown in you, because they will spring up, whether good or bad.

There is an interesting plant that exists in nature called the Belladonna, most commonly known as Deadly Nightshade. Ingestion of a single leaf from this plant can be fatal. Here's where it gets really interesting. Tomatoes, potatoes, and eggplant grow out of the very same family of this poisonous plant. How does this apply to you?

Just because you have come out of a bad situation, or a sordid past, you don't have to become what you came out of. You do not have to allow the deadly poison of negative experiences and toxic influences to become a part of you. Because if they do, you will not feel worthy enough, or capable enough, to accept God's calling. You can overcome past failures, bad relationships, and poor choices. Even if someone you loved left you, and it hurt, you can still overcome. Don't stop living. Don't let your past steal your future.

Declare this over your life: *That was then, but this is now. I am victorious in Christ Jesus. I am not defeated because the Lord is on my side. He has a call on my life. He has already told me what I will become. No one and nothing can stop what God has for me.*

When you begin talking like that, you build up your faith. You strengthen your resolve. You motivate yourself. You begin feeling happier, stronger, and more optimistic about your future.

It is paramount that you begin thinking more positively, because if you don't, you will succumb to a defeatist mentality. It is easy to fall into a pessimistic attitude and that can cause you to start to believe that nothing will ever work out for you. As a result, you may come to expect defeat and rejection. You may expect to be disliked and ridiculed. Before you realize it, you can grow a poisonous garden full of Belladonnas where your strength is compromised only of negativity. That toxicity can permeate your psyche and prohibit your productivity.

Earl Nightingale, a great thinker and philosopher, shares a profound truth in a famous recording called, "The Strangest Secret" (Nightingale Conant, audio-book, 1976).

> The human mind is much like a farmer's land. The land gives the farmer a choice. He may plant in that land whatever he chooses. The land doesn't care what is planted. It's up to the farmer to make the decision. The mind, like the land, will return what you plant,

but it doesn't care what you plant. If the farmer plants two seeds—one, a seed of corn...the other nightshade, a deadly poison...it will return poison in just as wonderful abundance as it will corn. So up come the two plants—one corn, one poison...as it's written in the Bible, 'As ye sow, so shall ye reap.'

Isn't that powerful? You have the ability to choose what type seeds are planted in the soil of your spirit. Get rid of the Deadly Nightshade that has left you believing you are not good enough, not smart enough, not gifted enough, not attractive enough, or not valuable enough. You can overcome these negative thoughts and influences by breaking free in your thinking. You may feel that I cannot possibly understand the depth of your hurt. I was not there when it all went down and I don't know about all the nights you soaked your pillow with tears. And you are exactly right. I do not know the intricate details of your particular situation, but God does. He knows if you have been abused, mistreated, or misunderstood. He knows that if beneath the surface of that smile there is a wound you aren't sure will ever be healed. But it can and by His power, it will.

Old wounds, when left unchecked, fester and grow. The negativity eats away at your sense of worth and poisons your mind. This prohibits you from embracing the call of God on your life. From now on, when you are dealing with the leftover junk from past hurts and brokenness, "Don't nurse it...don't rehearse it...disperse it!" You must release all of that pent up resentment, anger, and hurt. It only leads to a poor self-image and low self-esteem.

When you carry wounds along with you, you don't need anyone to beat you down and mistreat you. When you do so you end up picking up where others left off. You kick yourself! You call yourself ugly! You call yourself stupid! You tell yourself that nobody will ever love you. Whatever you believe shapes and molds your circumstances. Begin to say what God says about you in His Word. You are more than a conqueror (Romans 8:37 NKJV). You are accepted in the beloved (Ephesians 1:6 NKJV). You are the righteousness of God in Christ Jesus (1 Corinthians 1:30 NKJV).

OVERCOME THE PRISON OF YOUR PAST

Moving beyond your negative past and embracing your positive future is more than a notion. It is not merely an exercise in positive thinking or behavioral modification. Change begins within and then manifests on the outside, not the other way around. Will power, personal affirmations, jumping up and down three times, and smacking your neighbor upside the head, is not going to change you. When you get finished leaping and coming down from your emotional high, you are still going to have to deal with your issues.

Can we get real for a minute? Each of us has learned to masquerade. Granted, some of us do it better than others, but we all know how to disguise our true feelings on some level. It is time to stop

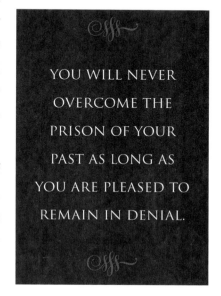

YOU WILL NEVER OVERCOME THE PRISON OF YOUR PAST AS LONG AS YOU ARE PLEASED TO REMAIN IN DENIAL.

concealing them and start dealing with them. You will never overcome the prison of your past as long as you are pleased to remain in denial. Until you stop denying that you have a problem, you can never receive help.

Getting past your past does not mean covering it up and acting like it never happened. Rather, it means being honest enough with God and yourself to admit that you are still walking around with unresolved issues. Perhaps, you are masking things you have not dealt with for years, things that happened to you when you were just a small child; things that were done to you by those you should have been able to trust; things that were said to you and about you, that broke your spirit; things you did wrong and are ashamed of; things you wish would never have happened.

Those issues are the very ones that God wants you to lay at His feet, so He can heal your brokenness. He wants you to get past your past. He knows all about it. He was watching silently and standing by, waiting for you to run into His arms. Even then, you were called and even now, God's desires for you have not changed.

Still, you struggle with your history. You can't seem to get over what people have said or done. Unfortunately, when you allow "ex-offenders" to monopolize your thoughts, they end up controlling your life. How then, can you go about the process of being released from their clutches? How can you truly be delivered? The answer is embodied in one word, forgiveness. You may not want to hear this, but it is so important. Do you know that you cannot overcome the prison of your past without forgiving those who did you wrong? I know you may not want to let it go. Holding onto the bitterness somehow feels like your consolation prize. But it's hindering you from fulfilling the call of God on your life.

When you allow the effect of a negative experience to take root in your heart, it robs you of your future. You become bitter, paranoid, suspicious, mistrustful, introverted, and afraid. Briefly read over those six adjectives again. Now ask yourself, "Do those sound like attributes that will hinder or help me, as I endeavor to accomplish God's will for my life?" You have to get to the core of the problem. You cannot do that, however, until you admit you are still carrying around extra baggage. There is no substitute for weeding things out from the root. Notice, you can't deal with the manifestation of the issue, without dealing with the origin of it. That would be putting the cart before the horse.

Sometimes it seems easier not to acknowledge certain hurts, especially when you have endured gross mistreatment, but it is not. I am reminded of the story of Tamar, King David's daughter (2 Samuel 13, NKJV). One of the most despicable incidents recorded in the Bible was when Amnon, a son of the king, found himself in a state of lustful infatuation with his young, virgin, half-sister, Tamar. Amnon concocted a scheme to lure her into his bed.

After she consistently rejected his advances, he forcibly violated her. Immediately after stealing her innocence, his "love" for her turned to loathing and contempt. Amnon said to her "Arise, be gone!" (13:15). Then he told his servant, "Here! Put this woman out, away from me, and bolt the door behind her" (13:17). She had no place of refuge or consolation. Even after Tamar's father, David, found out about it, although furious, he could do nothing to reverse the damage.

How do you recover when you have been mistreated and cast aside? How do you reconcile the wrong that has been done to you when those you thought would never hurt you do the unthinkable, and never apologize? Your experience may not be identical to Tamar's, but no doubt you have one. It may have been a time when you were wronged and no one stood up for you. Perhaps no one acknowledged what happened and you have been carrying it secretly, silently, and shamefully.

You don't have to walk around with your head hanging down. What happened to you does not undermine God's plan for your life. As Dr. Mike Murdock so appropriately says, "God does not consult your past to determine your future." Your dreams do not have to die. The hand of God is yet on your life. Even though others may have cast you aside, God is saying, "I still want you. You're still beautiful to Me. You're still valuable to Me. You're still significant to Me. I'll never throw you away."

You must understand that what Amnon did to Tamar was reprehensible. Even if the relationship had been consensual, it was against the law of God (Leviticus 18:11). After this tragic incident, the Bible says that Tamar placed ashes on her head as a symbol of mourning (2 Samuel 13:19). She agonized and grieved over what she had lost. What might you be grieving over? What are you mourning? What keeps you up at night? What secret are you holding?

You may not like to think about it or talk about it, but God cannot heal what you refuse to reveal. You do not have to stay behind your bolted prison door. God wants to set you free today! He wants to give you your life back. Stop walking around with guilt and shame. "There is therefore now no condemnation to those who are in Christ Jesus" (Romans 8:1a NKJV). I want you to know that you can, by the power of the Holy Spirit, overcome the prison of your past. God wants to renew your strength and restore your joy.

❧ EMBRACE YOUR FUTURE ❧

It's time now to press beyond your past and begin walking in your future. "...forgetting those things which are behind and reaching forward to those things which are ahead" (Philippians 3:13b NKJV). Hold your head up and know that you will use the lessons from your past to help you make a comeback. This time around you can come back stronger and wiser. Your past failures can be like your mentors. They remind you of what not to do. You are now equipped to move forward.

You have to break those shackles off your wrists. Completely release everything that has been holding you back. Get serious about it. Don't let the "ubiquitous they" control you any longer. Make up your mind that you are not carrying that junk around with you anymore. You've got work to do. God has plans for you. You have a calling to fulfill. Great things are just beyond the horizon. Can you sense the breaking of day? It is time for you to burst out of that little cell you've been locked up in.

You would not be reading this book unless you want to be a more productive person in the Kingdom of God. You want to walk in your purpose. You want to cast off restraints. You want to break out of your box. You want get past your past. You want to embrace your future. In Christ Jesus, you're free. There's nothing holding you, nothing blocking you, nothing restricting you...nothing but yourself. It's time to move forward.

Maybe you're wondering why I'm prompting you. Why am I pushing you to release those old hurts and negative seeds? To a great degree, I believe negativity is the enemy of productivity. Without releasing those old wounds, you won't ever move out of the confined space you currently occupy. They will keep you stuck in the past and limited in your perception. You won't be able to see the great and awesome things that you are capable of becoming in Christ Jesus. You will be yoked and shackled, unable to get free. In essence, you'll behave a lot like a trained elephant. Follow along while I expound upon this idea.

From the outset, the trainer begins conditioning the elephant's mind. It is taught from birth to remain confined to a very small space. To accomplish this, its leg is tied with a rope and attached to a wooden post. This post is planted very deeply in the ground, so it won't budge. The predetermined length of the rope dictates exactly how far the elephant can go. If it ever attempts to move beyond this designated space, it is yanked back by the force of the rope.

Initially, the young, vibrant elephant tries to break free of the restraints. It fights, jerks and tugs, but the rope is much too strong.

Eventually, the baby elephant comes to understand that it cannot break the rope, no matter how hard it tries. Rather than waste energy resisting, it learns to stay in its place.

As a result, the elephant that was once boisterous and stubborn becomes docile and submissive. It willingly abides within the parameters of the small space. By the time the elephant grows into a 5-ton colossus, it could easily snap that same rope. Yet, it does not even try. The reason being, it learned as a baby that the rope was unbreakable.

Are you like the elephant? Are you resigned to remain confined to your prison? Have you unwittingly been controlled by past hurts that limit your perspective? Have you settled for the small things in life: a small salary, a small business, a small ministry, a small platform, a small mentality? You cannot think small and expect big results. That is paradoxical. It is time to begin seeing yourself as God sees you. Awaken the

YOU CANNOT THINK SMALL AND EXPECT BIG RESULTS.

sleeping giant within. In order to thrive in your calling, you have got to get past your past, broaden your perspective, and yank yourself out of that rope.

It is your season to do bigger things for the Kingdom. Come out of that prison of small thinking. God is releasing you to embrace your future. You have cried, mourned, and agonized over your past long enough. Now God is saying, release it. It has been holding you back.

Release it. It has been keeping you confined. Release it. It has been causing you to doubt the call. Now is the time to break out of prison and walk in victory!

It is possible. Consider the apostle Peter. He was placed in prison by King Herod, under maximum security. Yet, when it was his season to be free, God sent an angel to release him. When the hour came for Peter's deliverance from prison, he did not even know it was coming. As a matter of fact, the angel showed up in the middle of the night while Peter was asleep (Acts 12:5–10). He wasn't necessarily expecting a miraculous prison break; nonetheless, I want you to know that when it's your time of breakthrough, it's just your time. God is about to release you into your destiny.

❧ GOD IS DOING A NEW THING ❧

God is preparing you for great things. The struggles of your past may have been tough, yet you are still here because God has a plan for your life. He is getting ready to do a new thing in you. What He is about to do through you is far greater than you have envisioned. "Do not remember the former things, Nor consider the things of old. Behold, I will do a new thing, Now it shall spring forth; shall you not know it?" (Isaiah 43:18-19 NKJV).

The blessing of the Lord is on your life. That is why He is urging you not to get bogged down by your past. In Acts 12:7, when the angel showed up in Peter's cell, he commanded him to get up quickly. Instantly, his chains fell off his hands. You, too, can "arise quickly." And the things that have kept you bound will fall off. God may elevate you sooner than you have anticipated. In an instant, He can turn things in your favor and unexpected blessings can flow your way.

You see, God knows just when to move on your behalf. He knows when you have had all you can take. I'm sure there have been times that you have felt like you were going to die in prison, but He already knew your release date. In the book of Exodus, the children of Israel were enslaved in the land of Egypt for over 400 years. God had not forgotten them. He already had a plan to bring them out. When the Lord appeared to Moses from the midst of the burning bush He said, "I have surely seen the oppression of My people who are in Egypt, and have heard their cry because of their taskmasters, for I know their sorrows. So I have come down to deliver them out of the hand of the Egyptians, and to bring them up from that land to a good and large land, to a land flowing with milk and honey…" (Exodus 3:7, 8a NKJV).

The Israelites were crying out to God. He already knew the means by which He would deliver them out of their bondage. Through your hardships and struggles, you've also been praying and crying out to God. He has not forgotten you. He will bring you out with a mighty hand. God has already worked things out on your behalf. Remember, you are His chosen one, selected to accomplish His purpose.

You can no longer let your past keep you tied up, because believe it or not, someone is depending on you for their deliverance. You may not realize it, but you are someone's answer. They need what you have inside of you. The longer it takes for you to recognize that, the longer it takes for them to be delivered by God, through you.

Understand, there is a void in the land that needs filling, and the world is waiting for the impact that only you have been destined and designed to make. It's time for you to rise to the occasion and demonstrate the true essence of your calling in the earth. Romans 8:19 says it this way, "For the earnest expectation of the creation eagerly waits for the revealing of the sons of God" (NKJV). The phrase, "earnest expectation" describes the act of waiting and watching with an outstretched neck. Get the picture? There are literally scores of people eagerly waiting for you to take your place and answer the call. Startling, perhaps, but their very lives are at stake.

When the Israelites were crying out to God for deliverance, He had already chosen Moses to fulfill the call. But Moses, the future deliverer, was struggling to break free from the prison of his own past. Notice the irony in this; the Israelites were in Egypt, longing for freedom. However, the very one who was appointed to carry out the assignment, had to first break free of his own limited thinking before he could execute what God had called him to do.

"But Moses said to God, 'Who am I that I should go to Pharaoh, and that I should bring the children of Israel out of Egypt?'"(Exodus 3:11 NKJV). Moses missed it. He was still stuck in the past. I can imagine that his mind wandered back to that day when, in a misguided attempt to help one of his kinsmen, he killed an Egyptian man and hid him in the sand (Exodus 2:12). Or perhaps Moses was haunted by the time when he attempted to make peace between two of his Hebrew brethren, only to be met with rejection, criticism, and ridicule. Let's take a closer look at what happened.

The Bible records, "...two Hebrew men were fighting, and he said to the one who did the wrong, 'Why are you striking your companion?' Then he said, 'Who made you a prince and a judge over us? Do you intend to kill me as you killed the Egyptian?'" (Exodus 2:13a, 14 NKJV). Ouch! I'm sure this incident had a deep psychological impact on Moses. After all, it was another failed attempt at helping his own people.

Aside from the obvious fear of losing his life for committing murder, Moses had to relive those thoughts that had been suppressed for so many years. He had to deal with the guilt he felt over what he had done wrong. Moses must have struggled with the idea that, in spite of his shortcomings, God still called Him out of the midst of that burning bush. Could God really want him? The murderer? The fugitive? That is exactly why you need to break free from the prison of your past right now. Otherwise, when God calls you out, you might be struggling, when you should be surrendering to His purpose and plan.

Breaking free in your mind is crucial. Not for God's sake, but for your own. God is in no way moved by your feelings of inadequacy and insecurity. You are the one for the job. He knows the plans He has laid out for you and they are not changing. You, on the other hand, will wrestle mentally with the call of God if you don't adjust your thinking. Accept the fact that He knows you through and through, and He still has not changed His mind about you. "The gifts

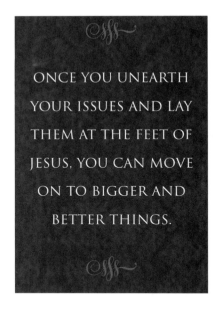

ONCE YOU UNEARTH YOUR ISSUES AND LAY THEM AT THE FEET OF JESUS, YOU CAN MOVE ON TO BIGGER AND BETTER THINGS.

and the calling of God are irrevocable" (Romans 11:29 NKJV). Now, take a deep breath. Straighten your back. Lift up your head. Walk right out of your past and into your future. Now look over your shoulder and wave goodbye.

You may be thinking it's not that simple. Yes it is. Once you unearth your issues and lay them at the feet of Jesus, you can move on to bigger and better things. Let Him have all those sorrows and hurts. "...casting all your care upon Him, for He cares for you" (1 Peter 5:7 NKJV). Remove the chains of your past from around your neck and make the switch. Jesus says, "Take My yoke upon you and learn from Me, for I am gentle and lowly in heart, and you will find rest for your souls. For My yoke is easy and My burden is light" (Matthew 11:29, 30 NKJV).

As you release the heavy burden that you have been carrying, you will be able to catch a glimpse of just how valuable you are to God. He loves you more than you know and He has called you for a purpose greater than you can imagine. "Before I formed you in the womb I knew you, before you were born I set you apart; I appointed you as a prophet to the nations..." (Jeremiah 1:5 NIV). You are dearly loved by God and He is going to use you for His glory.

You may be wondering what makes you worthy and what makes you so special. That realization is beyond you. It's God. In other words, you are significant because you belong to Him. Be encouraged today and begin confessing that you matter to God, but your past does not. I know the enemy tries to make you feel unworthy. Right now, pray that God will renew your mentality and help you to begin aligning your thoughts with His Word. Start seeing yourself as the mighty conqueror you are.

"Yet in all these things we are more than conquerors through Him who loved us" (Romans 8:37 NKJV). As you realize that your worth and value are not tied to your past, it will become much easier to fulfill your Divine calling. Before you move on to the next chapter, be sure to internalize the valuable lessons you have learned. Then, put them into practice in your daily walk.

CHAPTER 3

LOSE THE WEIGHT

Time to Shed a Few People

ANONYMOUS

Now that you understand how to get past your past, you are free to embrace your God given dreams and discover your real purpose. It is a time of celebration, but also a time of work. If you don't plan on getting locked up in prison all over again, you are going to have to make some serious changes. It's true. If you really want to stay free, get ready to lose the weight by shedding a few people.

The road ahead will not always be paved with praise, applause, and adulation from everyone around you. You are not likely to have a ticker-tape parade held in your honor. It is what it is. Some people will say you are not called or that your dream is crazy and it's never going to come to pass. Others will tell you that you don't have what it takes, you're bucking the system, and you're out of order. Let these people go. They are just dead weight and dead weight limits your mobility. People of this sort will hold you back if you don't cut them loose. You cannot afford to be pulled back into the mediocrity, repression, and confinement you have prayed so hard to be freed from. They are discouragers, scoffers, and cynics. Do not allow them to succeed, except in pushing you closer toward the goal of fulfilling your life's assignment.

YOU CANNOT DRAG LIABILITIES AROUND WITH YOU AND EXPECT TO MOVE FORWARD WITH YOUR LIFE.

You cannot drag liabilities around with you and expect to move forward with your life. By liabilities I mean anything or anyone that takes something away from you and does not add anything to you. Essentially, you have to shake off those people who attach themselves to you. Like leeches, they suck out the life blood of your extraordinary creativity and exceptional vitality.

This type of people do not want you to challenge the status quo, because they have settled into the sleepy solace of mediocrity. They do not wish to be jarred out of their comfort zones. But for them, it's too bad and it's too late. You have already used your "get-out-of-jail-free card" and you are walking into your destiny, whether they like it or not.

Be prepared, now that you're embracing the call of God on your life, you will become the object of unfair ridicule, simply because you dare to dream bigger and do better. Hold firmly to God's hand during this season, because releasing people who limit you is not always easy. I'm serving you notice. You are entering the place that causes many to succumb to their fears and negative pressures, and voluntarily return to their prison cells.

- It's the place where you lose friends you thought would always be with you.

- It's the place where you experience betrayal from those closest to you.

- It's the place where your most avid supporters suddenly disappear, leaving no forwarding address.

What place am I speaking of? It is the place of separation. Albeit painful, it's inescapable. Are you ready? Let's go.

SEPARATE SO YOU DON'T RECIDIVATE

You have got to decide who you will hold on to and who you will release. Otherwise, you are liable to slip right back into the same situation that got you locked up in the first place. Essentially, you will *recidivate,* which means, "to return to a negative pattern of behavior, most commonly, crime."

The national recidivism rate is extremely high for ex-offenders. How high? According to the US Department of Justice, Bureau of Justice Statistics, "2 out of 3 inmates re-offend within 3 years of their release from prison" (http://www.ojp.usdoj.gov/bjs/reentry/recidivism.htm). That's a staggering statistic and it has everything to do with human behavior. If you have just been released from the prison of your past, you still have some work to do to stay free.

Just as many ex-offenders re-offend, you too, run the risk of going right back into your own prison, unless you change your influences. Get rid of the dead weight. You cannot continue to hang around people who are still bound and chained and expect that you will stay free. You absolutely must align yourself with new associations and connections. That way, you will not recidivate into old behaviors, old ways of thinking, and old ways of living. Guard your liberation. The opportunity to return to your former bondage is always lurking just around the corner. You must separate, so you don't recidivate.

"Stand fast therefore in the liberty by which Christ has made us free, and do not be entangled again with a yoke of bondage" (Galatians 5:1 NKJV). Remaining free from the yoke of bondage and walking in your newfound liberty happens by choice, not by chance. You have to choose to be free. In Galatians 5, Paul was trying to help the Galatians remain liberated from the bondage of the law, but they were having a crisis of conscience. On one hand, it was wonderful to know their salvation was not based on works or personal merit. On the other hand, the Galatians had legalistic Jewish teachers, also known as Judaizers, who influenced them. They kept telling them they needed to be circumcised in order to keep God's covenant that He had established with Abraham (Genesis 17:10-14).

The problem was not with circumcision in and of itself. The Law was, is, and always will be holy and right. The issue was the Judaizers were telling people that in order to be truly saved, they had to be circumcised and conform to other Jewish rituals and customs. Paul knew better. He was not willing to stand idly by, while others were being taught that salvation was attained by works. This erroneous teaching contradicted and undermined the redemptive work of Christ on the cross. "For by grace you have been saved through faith, and that not of yourselves; it is the gift of God, not of works, lest anyone should boast" (Ephesians 2:8, 9 NKJV).

Unfortunately, the Galatians had too many traditionalists controlling them. Isn't it interesting, when you make the decision to respond to God's call, seemingly everybody around you hears from God on your behalf? Everyone's got a word, a revelation, a dream, or a warm tingling sensation, that must be the Holy Ghost. Amazingly, they know exactly what you should be doing and how you should be doing it. The problem is, what they say directly contradicts what God is saying. Who are you going to trust? It's an either or decision, either them or God. It's your call.

Don't be surprised. When God is doing a new work in your life, there will always be narrow-minded traditionalists trying to rob you of your freedom. They will speak against what He is doing, because they don't understand it. They will tell you every reason why you cannot carry out the vision God has placed in your heart. Some will even pull out the Bible and use Scripture out of context, to back up their claims. Just

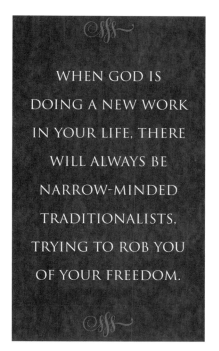

WHEN GOD IS DOING A NEW WORK IN YOUR LIFE, THERE WILL ALWAYS BE NARROW-MINDED TRADITIONALISTS, TRYING TO ROB YOU OF YOUR FREEDOM.

stay focused and accept the Father's will. Opposition is a part of the process of discovering your life's purpose.

Evaluate your own life. Who is always telling you that you can't? Who are the people that consistently say you are wrong and out of order? Be careful not to let them do to you what the Judaizers did to some of the Galatians. They ultimately caused them to depend upon the works of the law to make them righteous, rather than placing their faith in the completed work of Christ.

You cannot rely on the counsel of those who are bound to help you get free. That's a paradox. They cannot tell you anything about freedom when they are enslaved themselves. They do not understand it. Until you stop listening to closed-minded individuals, you will never be open-minded enough to fully embrace your calling. What God is instructing you to do may be viewed as too radical.

Resist those who cause you to regress, retreat, or rehash the past that God has already delivered you from. I cannot stress enough the importance of getting the dead weight off you. God has called you to do amazing things, but you run the risk of getting locked up all over again if you don't let some people go.

Let's be honest. Bondage did not just jump on your back one day out of the clear blue. It set in over time. Something may have happened and you did not forgive. You may have gotten hurt and you did not deal with it. There may be toxic people who have latched onto you and you have not shaken them off. Dominant people may have controlled you and you did not stand up for yourself. Perfidious people, or as we say, "two-faced folks", may have lied to you, and you let it slide. Maybe even God has tried to get your attention, but you did not listen. Wise advisors may have told you, "They mean you no good," but perhaps you pushed ahead anyway. As time progressed, those unhealthy people and situations became strongholds in your life.

It is only by the grace of God that you are here now. Even if you got yourself tied up in some big mess, God saw fit to deliver you with a mighty hand. You know I'm telling the truth. Consequently, you have to be extra careful about the people you allow into your life. It's one thing to break free; it's another thing to stay free. You have been delivered, but the enemy is seeking to devour you. He wants nothing more than to see you locked up and confined once more.

The enemy knows as long as you stay free, then you'll set other people free. As long as you continue to shake off what once held you back, he can't keep you contained. You are a mighty force for the Kingdom of the Almighty God. The enemy has a bounty on your head, but God in you is greater.

When the enemy sees your house in order, he looks for a place to infiltrate. If you haven't fortified your spirit, he is going to get back in. He will bring that same joker that you got tied up with before. The phone will ring and on the other end will be that voice that makes you weak in the knees. You better hang up that phone. Better yet, get your number changed. You had to go through too much to get free. You may have lost everything messing around with the wrong people. You don't have time to be playing around. If you let yourself get careless again, guess what? Back to prison you go. It is time to lose the weight of negative influences.

❧ GET OUT OF THE CHICKEN COOP ❧

"You must constantly ask yourself these questions: Who am I around? What are they doing to me? What have they got me reading? What have they got me saying? Where do they have me going? What do they have me thinking? And most important, what do they have me becoming? Then ask yourself the big question: Is that okay? Your life does not get better by chance, it gets better by change." (Jim Rohn, American Speaker and Author)

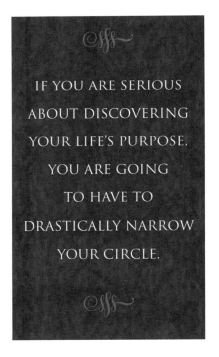

IF YOU ARE SERIOUS ABOUT DISCOVERING YOUR LIFE'S PURPOSE, YOU ARE GOING TO HAVE TO DRASTICALLY NARROW YOUR CIRCLE.

Association breeds assimilation. The people you spend the most time with are your greatest influences. If you are serious about discovering your life's purpose, you are going to have to drastically narrow your circle. Some people keep you restricted to a small mentality, simply because they don't have bigger visions for their own lives. There's a simple story that perfectly illustrates my point.

Once upon a time, there was a large mountainside where an eagle's nest rested. The eagle's nest contained four large eagle eggs. One day an earthquake rocked the mountain causing one of the eggs to roll down the mountainside into a chicken farm, located in the valley below. The farmer wanted to protect and care for the eagle's egg, so he nurtured the egg.

Finally one day, the egg hatched and a beautiful eagle was born. That eagle was raised to be a chicken. He ate what the chickens ate. He flapped his wings like the chickens, but never got very high off the ground. As time went on, the eagle believed he *was* a chicken. After all, that was all he had ever seen. The eagle grew comfortable with his home and family. Until one day, he looked up into the skies above and noticed a group of mighty eagles soaring.

"Wow!" the eagle cried, "I wish I could soar like those birds up there!" When the chickens heard it, they roared with laughter and said, "You cannot soar with those birds silly. *They* are eagles and *you* are a chicken, and chickens do not soar." The eagle continued staring into the sky, wishing he could soar with those eagles. Each time he would talk about his dreams of one day flying, the chickens would laugh mockingly and tell him, it couldn't be done.

Eventually the eagle learned to accept his life as a chicken and stopped dreaming of anything more. After a long life as a chicken, the eagle passed away, never knowing he could fly.

I know that is a simple story, but the lesson contained in it is so profound. If you keep hanging around chickens, you will eventually assimilate to that lifestyle and never tap into your purpose. The longer you dwell among chickens, the more you identify with their mentalities, philosophies, and sense of complacency. You slowly lose more and more of yourself until you end up forfeiting your calling. If you are committed to discovering your life's purpose, then you are going to have to make some drastic changes.

Are you willing to release everything and everybody that is a hindrance in your life? It's your call. It's easy to say, "I'm ready. I want all God has for me." However, when the rubber meets the road, are you really ready to do what it takes to break the bonds of limiting beliefs, behaviors, and barriers? Are you really willing to get out of the chicken coop and soar?

❧ THE TRAP OF MEDIOCRITY ❧

During this season, you are going to have to make sure that you associate with people who are qualified to influence your thinking. Everyone does not have the right mentality. Some people will stomp all over your dreams. They don't necessarily mean any harm; they just don't know any better. Albert Einstein said it this way, "Great spirits have always encountered violent opposition from mediocre minds."

Earlier in this chapter, we talked about traditionalists and legalistic people who refuse to embrace the new thing that God is doing. Now,

"IF YOU WANT SOMETHING YOU'VE NEVER HAD, YOU'VE GOT TO DO SOMETHING YOU'VE NEVER DONE."

we are dealing with the people who are addicted to mediocrity. They are perfectly satisfied doing the same unproductive things they have always done. They enjoy being chickens. You cannot stay with them. Like the Prodigal Son, you must come to yourself and arise from where you are (Luke 15: 17, 18).

It's time to make some changes and getting rid of procrastination is great place to start. You know the saying, "If you want something you've never had, you've got to do something you've never done." If you want to fulfill your calling, change your company. You can't drive under the influence of chickens.

People who are complacent, comfortable, and careless in their approach to life are not going to help push you to the place God wants you to go. You might know some of those usual suspects that are still doing what they've always done—nothing. They are the ones who don't plan on changing. They are still hanging out all night and sleeping all day. They are still talking about being rich, but won't get a job. They are still blaming the system for all of their woes, but won't lift a finger to complete their education. You can't hang around chickens and expect to soar like an eagle. It just won't work.

In order to maximize your opportunity to live abundantly, you need to be around other eagles. Renew your mind, nourish your soul, and fortify your spirit. Eagles are found faithfully attending worship services, praying, reading the Word of God, and staying as far away from their old coops as possible. Eagles know that there is nothing going on in the chicken coop that wasn't going on 10 years ago when they left. Some people don't want to do better and will get frustrated with you for trying. The sooner you accept the fact that everyone can't go with you, the easier it will be to release the dead weight.

Consider it from this perspective: you cannot fit the same clothes you wore when you were an infant. You have grown, but the clothes are still the same size. You have outgrown them. The same applies to people and relationships. You have matured. They have not. The relationship is not a good fit anymore. Why would you try to squeeze yourself into a mold that does not fit? It may not even be that you and the other person have grown apart. The other person just stopped growing.

Many people who used to be close to you aren't anymore, because they have not moved forward. As you continue to feed your mind and your spirit with God's Word, you may find that you have very little in common with the people of your past. They will no longer be on your level and that is okay. It doesn't mean you don't love them. It doesn't mean that you think you're better than them, not at all. It just means that you are not willing to remain in the chicken coop with them at the expense of your purpose.

Never feel guilty about growing and advancing. Don't let complacent individuals keep you restricted to that old way of thinking. Everybody has choices. If they have chosen to stay where they are that is not your responsibility. Since you have chosen to move toward where God wants you to be, rather than trying to appease those old friends, release them. Release that dead weight. They will not be adding anything to you anymore. They're time wasters.

You don't have time to hang out, just to be hanging out with people who will drag you down. You don't have time to sit on the phone and engage in mindless chatter. You don't need to hear the latest gossip. You have outgrown them and they don't fit in your life anymore. Just like a pair of shoes that are too small, the conversation is uncomfortable and downright painful sometimes. Your ideas and their ideas clash. You are both at complete opposite ends of the spectrum. If they say left, you say, right. If they say, no, you say, yes. You don't agree. "Can two walk together, unless they are agreed?" (Amos 3:3 NKJV).

You are an eagle. Get out of the chicken coop. That phase of your life is over. Your old alliances are no longer suitable. Those particular individuals are content to remain in the same place. They don't mind the situation they are in, but you are changing. Your goals are different and your mentality is different. You cannot take them with you. What's more, they don't want to go.

LOSE THEM, BUT HOLD ON TO YOUR DREAMS

Some people and even family members are dream killers. You can recognize them by the way they speak and the way they treat you. They are repeatedly negative and speak defeat over your dreams. You can't take dream killers along with you, because overexposure to their toxic thinking will adversely affect your mentality. Bad company corrupts good manners (1 Corinthians 15:33). Check your friends. Check your associations. Check your family. Make sure they are not feeding you Deadly Nightshade. Don't receive their words of death and defeat over your life and don't let them control you.

BAD COMPANY CORRUPTS GOOD MANNERS.

How exactly do dream killers control you? They appoint themselves governors and rulers over your thoughts, ideas, and actions. They work to silence your dreams and make you subservient, subordinate, and submissive. They try to shut your mouth so you won't speak your dreams. They try to control your mind so you won't believe your dreams. Finally, they try to prohibit your actions so you won't pursue your dreams.

They may tell you that being confident is being arrogant; talking about what you will accomplish in the future is boasting; your unwillingness to hang out in the chicken coop is mean spirited; your refusal to be governed by the status quo is rebellion; and your desire to live the good life is carnality. You have to release these dream killers. Naturally, once they control what you think, they automatically control what you do. Dr. Carter G. Woodson puts it like this in his book, *The Mis-Education of the Negro:*

> When you control a man's thinking you do not have to worry about his actions. You do not have to tell him not to stand here or go yonder. He will find his 'proper place' and will stay in it. You do not need to send him to the back door. He will go without being told. In fact, if there is no back door, he will cut one for his special benefit. His education makes it necessary. (Trenton: Africa World Press, 1990)

Although Dr. Woodson was directly addressing the residual effects of the enslavement of African American people in the United States, the essence of the message is broadly applicable. At the core of his argument is the power of mental conditioning. That is to say, once you become accustomed to a particular way of thinking, good or bad, you act out those behaviors in your manner of living. That is why it is so important to keep your space cleared of dream killers. Otherwise, you may internalize their negativism, pessimism, and cynicism. You could begin thinking, "Perhaps they're right. Maybe I am being ridiculous. Maybe I am just a chicken. Maybe I'm not really called." Before you know it, you could happily climb back into a little box, once again, held captive by the prison of your thinking.

Take time now to evaluate your relationships. Do you have a dream killer? If so, you have to make a decision. You can release the dream killers or turn back, put the yoke of bondage around your neck, and grow comfortable in your tiny cell. Cutting off a relationship can be a difficult thing but the day of decision is here. What are you going to do? This is where strong men grow weak and determined women grow weary. Why? No one wants to face the intense ridicule, rejection, and resentment from their peers, but keeping your dreams alive is worth it!

When you refuse to be oppressed, repressed, and suppressed; those who want to keep you confined will not be rejoicing, but don't focus on them. Focus on the work that God is doing in you and it is a good work indeed (Philippians 1:6). He is retraining and reconditioning your thinking. He's remolding and reshaping your perception of yourself. Those who have tried to keep you bound will by no means celebrate your liberty. Don't fall victim to them. You have a choice. Being free is a choice.

You have the freedom to carve out a new path.
The freedom to be who God says you are.

The freedom to express your creativity.

The freedom to say no!

The freedom to break the cycle that has been in your family for years.

The freedom to take the road less traveled.

The freedom to get away from the dream killers.

Those who stifle your creativity and make you second guess yourself will teach you to be insecure and passive. That is not who you are. God has given you a mind of your own. You have opinions, preferences, and God-given ideas. It may seem simpler to go along with the old crowd and pretend not to feel the frustration of hanging around the chicken coop. It may seem easier when you know you're called to be an eagle, to suppress your dreams, rather than, deal with ridicule. Now, you may think I'm just being cynical and negative, but that's not so. Let's look at the life of Joseph.

When he gave voice to the dreams that God put in his heart, he experienced great persecution. "Now Joseph had a dream, and he told it to his brothers; and they hated him even more. So he said to them 'Please hear this dream which I have dreamed: There we were, binding sheaves in the field, Then behold, my sheaf arose and also stood upright; and indeed your sheaves stood all around and bowed down to my sheaf'" (Genesis 37:5-7 NKJV).

Everyone cannot handle your dreams. I don't recommend that you go around indiscriminately sharing what the Lord has shown you. Some things you should just keep to yourself or share with those you trust. Let me also point out, though, Joseph's brothers hated him well before he mentioned this dream. They despised Joseph, because their father, Jacob, favored him above them all (Gen.37: 3–4). In some cases, people do not like you just because you are favored by the Father. There is nothing you can do about that except to pray.

We know Joseph's dream was prophetic. As ruler in Egypt, he would eventually save his family from being ravaged by famine. At the time, however, the implication of his dream was nothing more than an insult to his brothers. They were incensed. "And his brothers said to him, 'Shall you indeed reign over us? Or shall you indeed have dominion over us?' So they hated him even more for his dreams and for his words" (Genesis 37:8 NKJV). The problem was that Joseph's dream violated custom. The firstborn was considered the prominent one in the family and he was the youngest. It seemed like Joseph was just talking crazy. Sometimes, what God has in store for you will break the back of tradition. Everyone will not be ready to deal with it, so just be quiet until God releases you.

In Genesis 37:9-11, we see Joseph sharing another dream in which the sun, the moon and the eleven stars bowed down to him. This time, he upset the whole family. His father, Jacob, rebuked him and his brothers envied him even more. However, Jacob did not dismiss what Joseph shared. I can imagine he sensed that God really was dealing with the boy. Though Joseph lacked wisdom, he by no means lacked revelation. By this point, his dreams had exacerbated an already contentious relationship with his brothers. Now, they were intent on silencing him and those offensive dreams, once and for all (Genesis 37:23–28).

Oftentimes, the dream killers will be those closest to you. The very ones who should love and protect you could quickly turn on you. They may resent you, because you are embracing God's calling and pursuing your purpose. Perhaps, you think, if you silence your dreams it will take care of the problem. While I do believe you should use wisdom and diplomacy, keeping quiet is not going to make dream killers despise you any less. Joseph's brothers hated him because he was favored. The dreams only added insult to injury. He couldn't make himself dream, they came from the Lord.

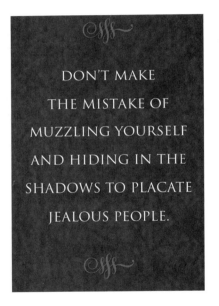

DON'T MAKE THE MISTAKE OF MUZZLING YOURSELF AND HIDING IN THE SHADOWS TO PLACATE JEALOUS PEOPLE.

Stop thinking it's always your fault when people resent you. It's not. There is nothing you will ever be able to do to appease a dream killer. Your very presence repulses them. You ruin their whole day when you show up. Your contagious zeal for life irritates them. Whether you speak your dreams or remain silent, the call to greatness on your life is obvious to all who see you. Don't make the mistake of muzzling yourself and hiding in the shadows to placate jealous people.

By subverting your dreams and abandoning your call to make others happy, you will find yourself unfulfilled. Worse yet, you will never seize your destiny. Don't diminish your personhood to pacify those who are envious of the gift of God within you. Certainly, you *can* attempt to appease them. Still, after you do all that compromising, they won't like you. Why? Your purpose speaks, even when you are silent. The favor of God is on you, so embrace it. Say yes to your call and no to dream killers.

Whoever they may be, let them go. Stop trying to be something you're not. You are an eagle and it's time to stop trying to fit in with chickens. They may tolerate you, but they will never celebrate you. They may laugh with you, then turn around and laugh at you. They may talk to you and then talk about you. Meanwhile, you are trying to overcompensate to make them feel better about you and themselves. It won't work.

When they reject you, just dust your shoulders off and know that there is a throne waiting for you. There is a place where people will honor the anointing of God on your life. The individuals you are assigned to will appreciate your gifts and talents. Joseph's place was Egypt. God also has a place for you, but you must release those dream killers first. Tell yourself that you will be all that God called you to be. Point to yourself and say:

I won't let my dreams die.
I will do all God has called me to do.
I will not leave this earth until I have discovered and fulfilled
my purpose.
So what if they don't like me.
So what if they talk about me.
So what if they reject me.
I will not abort my dreams.
God gave them to me.

God will empower you to endure this season. He will give you strength to stand firmly while you are being repositioned and realigned. He has called you out from among the chickens so that you can soar. As you lose them, you will begin to find yourself. Stop trying to keep unhealthy people around for their approval. You want to be accepted, loved, and embraced, however, you must realize that true friends never require that you subvert your dreams or change who you are to be accepted. People who are envious and jealous are not worth having around. They are liabilities. Let them go.

I pray, even as you're reading, that God will begin to reveal the hidden identity of the dream killers in your life. They're under cover. They've been smiling in your face, but their hearts were never with you. You have already lost too much of yourself trying to keep them. Release them. This may be one of the hardest things you have ever had to do, but release them anyhow. You might even shed some tears, but release them. You believe that you need them, but God is saying you don't need them at all.

Dream killers hinder the vision God has implanted in your heart and He desires for the separation to happen so His will and purpose will be accomplished in you. Even in the story of Joseph, when all was said and done, he realized that being separated from his family was actually God's doing all the time. He said, "And God sent me before you to preserve a posterity for you in the earth, and to save your lives by a great deliverance. So now it was not you who sent me here, but God…" (Genesis 45:7, 8a NKJV). God's hand is all in this.

It is time for them to go and as you cut them loose, you will make room for God to do new and more awesome things in your life.

It is critical to identify the dead weight and dream killers in your life. Think about it for a while. Perhaps, you have lots of memories with them, old yearbook pictures and funny stories. Maybe they introduced you to your spouse. Possibly, they have known you since you were a baby. Think about those people who should support you, but get noticeably perturbed when you share good news. Seriously, ponder it right now.

Be wary of the best friend who suddenly turns on you when you get engaged; or your relatives and acquaintances who don't like you, once you get your degree and start to make a little money; or members of your local church assembly who will not speak to you when you are elevated to a new position; or peers who refuse to congratulate you on your new home; or people who never come to your most important events, or they come, but always find a way to interject something negative. They may say things like:

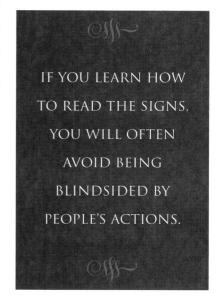

IF YOU LEARN HOW TO READ THE SIGNS, YOU WILL OFTEN AVOID BEING BLINDSIDED BY PEOPLE'S ACTIONS.

The house is nice, but it's too small. The car is nice, but the color is ugly. You look nice, but you've put on some weight. God is blessing, but don't get too haughty, because the storm is just around the corner. You're talking about starting a business, but you know, most businesses fail within the first five years.

Recognize the people in your life who keep you confined, because the signs are always there. You just have to open up your eyes and pay attention. Joseph's brothers hated him and they had a terrible time hiding it. The Bible says, "...they hated him and could not speak peaceably to him" (Genesis 37:4b). If you learn how to read the signs, you will often avoid being blindsided by people's actions. Usually, the relationship gradually turns sour. They say something and you wonder, "What did they mean by that?"

Instead of being happy for you, they say, "I don't know...you've just been acting funny lately. You're different. You think you're better than everybody else. You're just phony. All you think about is yourself. I know you're busy, but you could at least call or come by." But they haven't called you in the past year either! It's these people that you need to send packing.

It is a waste of your time to end up trying to figure out if you really have been acting phony or thinking maybe you are stuck on yourself. Maybe you are too arrogant. Maybe you do need to take time away from ministry, school, and work, to see about them. Before you start making adjustments and rearranging your life to make them more comfortable, consider this. You cannot afford to dedicate yourself and your time to mundane, nonproductive, time-wasting dream killers. You need to be spending those precious moments pursuing the call of God on your life.

It is a trick of the enemy to keep you responding to false emergencies and addressing problems that you should be avoiding in the first place. Instead of feeding into toxic people, spend more time in God's presence. Seek Him daily for His will. Enjoy your family. Focus on growing your business. Pursue your passion relentlessly. And ignore them.

Live a life of purpose and don't worry about people Satan has assigned to keep you off track. Today, make a decision. Will it be the chicken coop or the eagle's nest? The choice is yours.

CHAPTER 4

TAKE THE HEAT

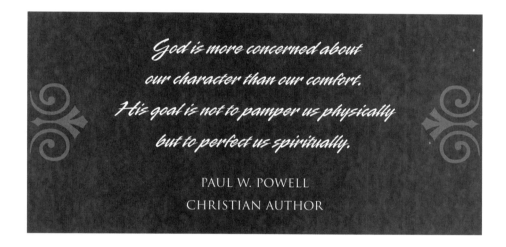

God is more concerned about our character than our comfort. His goal is not to pamper us physically but to perfect us spiritually.

PAUL W. POWELL
CHRISTIAN AUTHOR

Are you ready to be used by God? Are you prepared to vanquish demonic forces and triumphantly conquer the powers of darkness? Even if you do not feel completely prepared, God is currently recruiting ambassadors for His Kingdom and He has His own training program. You may need to undergo some refining, but you should be just fine. Before we move forward, we will establish a foundation to help you understand God's refining process.

"He *is* like a refiner's fire, and like fullers' soap: And he shall sit as a refiner and a purifier of silver: and he shall purify the sons of Levi, and purge them as gold and silver, that they may offer unto the LORD an offering in righteousness" (Malachi 3:2b, 3).

The sons of Levi mentioned in Malachi 3:3 represent the Old Testament Levitical Priesthood. They were men consecrated by God to act as intermediaries on behalf of the people by presenting offerings and sacrifices unto Him. Likewise, by the grace of God, you and I are now "accepted in the Beloved" (Ephesians 1:6 NKJV). As such, we are also " a chosen generation, a royal priesthood, a holy nation, His own special people, that you may proclaim the praises of Him who called you out of darkness into His marvelous light" (1 Peter 2:9 NKJV).

Our Father desires that we bring glory to His name; He meticulously molds us into vessels of honor, by removing anything in us that is contrary to His Divine nature.

LET GOD REFINE YOUR DESIGN

There is a great story I want to share with you to help you gain a clear view of how the Master Refiner does His work.

One day during a home-based youth Bible study, a young woman was puzzled about the Biblical depiction of God as "a refiner's fire and purifier of silver." So, she asked her peers, "Exactly what does that mean?"

Some of the attendees tried to explain it, however, the young woman was still confused about it. She wondered what the statement indicated about the character and nature of God. Well, another young woman got a great idea. She gleefully said, "Oh, I know! How about I visit a silversmith and observe the actual process of refining silver? I'll report my findings to the group at the next Bible Study."

Everyone thought it was an exceptional idea, so they all agreed. The very next day, the eager young woman called all over town to find an available silversmith, with no success. She was growing a little discouraged, because many of the local silversmiths were too busy to accommodate her request. She was just about ready to give up, when she decided to call the last number on her list. Lo and behold, a friendly old man answered the phone.

The young woman stammered on the other end, certain that he would say "no," just as all the others had. She hesitantly said, "Uh…hello, sir. I was wondering if it wouldn't be too much trouble for me to see how you do your work." To her surprise, the friendly old man was more than happy to make an appointment to let her watch him work the next day.

When she arrived, she didn't bother to mention anything about the reason for her interest in his work, beyond her curiosity about the process of refining silver. As the young woman settled in and quietly watched, the silversmith held a piece of silver over the fire and let it heat up. He explained in a loud warm tone, "You see child, when refining silver, you've got to hold the silver right in the middle of the fire where the flames are the hottest."

"Why?" asked the young woman.

"Well, the heat has to be hot enough to burn away all the impurities," replied the silversmith.

When she heard that, the young woman smiled, as she thought about some of the *hot spots* she had been in over the past few months, and how God must've been holding her there to help her all along. At that moment, she thought again about the verse that says, "He sits as a refiner and purifier of silver." Then, feeling a little more comfortable, she asked the silversmith,

"Is it true that you have to sit here in front of the fire the *whole time* the silver is being refined?"

"Why, yes child," answered the old man. He paused for a moment and then he said,

"I don't just sit here *holding* the silver, but I have to keep my eyes on the silver the entire time it's in the fire, because if the silver is left for just one moment too long in the flames, it'll be destroyed."

Wow! thought the young woman. She was silent again for a long while, pondering all she was learning. Then, she furrowed her brows and tilted her head, as she thought of another question. The young woman said, "Well, I just have one more question."

"What is it?" said the old man, as a broad smile now softened his face.

"How do you know when the silver is fully refined?"

He chuckled softly and answered, "Oh, that's quite easy, my dear … when I see my image in it. That's how I know."

If you have ever wondered why you must experience fiery trials, intense tribulation, and painful chastisement in your walk with the Lord, this is your answer. It is because God Himself, the Purifier, is using them to cleanse your character and mold your mentality. He wants you to reflect His image. Now, some people say that, "Trials make you strong." But I believe the *Word of God* you stand on *through* the trials, ultimately strengthens you. If you have been enduring some "hot spots" of your own, don't worry. Trust God's Word. Though you feel the intensity of the heat, you will not be consumed. Know that it is necessary and beneficial to your spiritual growth and development.

Without a doubt, as He's getting you ready for your platform, you will find yourself in the middle of some uncomfortable tests. Try to keep in mind during these periods of rebuke and chastisement that He's perfecting you for His glory. Don't be discouraged. "My son, do not despise the chastening of the LORD, Nor be discouraged when you are rebuked by Him; For whom the LORD loves He chastens, And scourges every son whom He receives" (Hebrews 12:5b,6 NKJV). Just know that when you come through this, you will be better for having humbly accepted His correction.

The late Reverend James Cleveland used to sing a Gospel song some years ago, along with Albertina Walker that says, "Please be patient with me, God is not through with me yet. When God gets through with me, I shall come forth as pure gold!"

Singing the lyrics to that song is one thing, but enduring the actual purification process is quite different. Prepare your mind for the journey ahead. Have you ever heard someone say, "If you can't stand the heat, get out of the kitchen?" Although it's a catchy quote, it's not an option for the Kingdom-minded. The heat is the very thing that causes all of our hidden impurities to rise to the surface. To run away from the heat is to run away from His will. In fact,

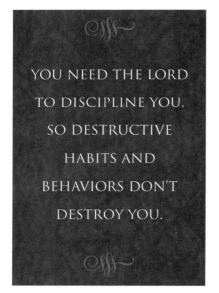

YOU NEED THE LORD TO DISCIPLINE YOU. SO DESTRUCTIVE HABITS AND BEHAVIORS DON'T DESTROY YOU.

running from the heat really just *slows* your pace. You will find out sooner or later that what you tried to avoid, you will encounter again and what you attempted to run away from, you will eventually run into.

Trust me when I say, I know God's method of preparing you to accomplish His purpose in the earth is often unpleasant. It may involve some pain and affliction of the flesh, but as a more apt saying goes, "What's good *for* you, doesn't always feel good *to* you." You need the Lord to discipline you, so destructive habits and behaviors don't destroy you. If you are honest, you'll admit that you have made some bad choices. On occasion, you may have taken yourself out of alignment with His will. All of us can testify to that. God, our loving Father, steps in and chastises us, so we will learn to bring our flesh under subjection and get back on track. Though it hurts, it is for our good.

"Now no chastening seems to be joyful for the present, but painful; nevertheless, afterward it yields the peaceable fruit of righteousness to those who have been trained by it" (Hebrews 12:11 NKJV). While God is doing His work, sometimes everything in you will cry out against the process. That's perfectly normal, because the last thing your carnal flesh wants to do is submit to the authority of God. "Because the carnal mind *is* enmity against God; for it is not subject to the law of God, nor indeed can be" (Romans 8:7 NKJV). We must rely on the power of God to help keep this old flesh in line.

Understand that He does not enjoy seeing you squirm; neither does He derive some twisted pleasure from your discomfort. Rather, He reproves you to improve you. While you are being sternly disciplined, however, it may not feel like real love.

My mind goes back to when I was a youngster coming up. My mother believed in corporal punishment or more commonly known by the "spank-ee" as "a beatin'." Her motto was "Hard heads make for soft behinds." She was anointed and appointed to lay hands on me suddenly—a direct violation of Scripture, might I add (1 Timothy 5:22). Of course that Scripture is not referring to spanking your children, but if I could have used it to get out of the spanking, I would have!

Like Muhammad Ali, she could "float like a butterfly and sting like a bee." I remember many days, lying prostrate at her feet, having been slain by *her* spirit. Lord have mercy please ... I think I just got a flashback! I can still clearly hear her saying, "I don't beat clothes." I don't even have to elaborate on that one. Sometimes, I didn't know if I would make it out alive. I felt like I was being beaten to death, but I'm still here, praise God, by His grace. Don't get me wrong in all this jesting. My mother never abused her children. Anyway, if she had, the statute of limitations prevents me from any type of latent recourse.

My mother would say things like, "This is going hurt me more than it hurts you," or "I'm doing this because I love you." Now, I remember thinking, "Uh…you know Mommy…I think there are much better ways to express your love for me. I have a few pretty good ideas. How about…you buy me some toys, take me to the amusement park and let's ride a rollercoaster, or just…not beat me." That's what was on my mind, although I never uttered those words. I possessed a deep reverential fear of my mother. Often, I stood in awe of her power and might while thinking, "This woman is seriously crazy. I had better obey if I want to see the light of day."

She taught me to walk upright and she kept me on the straight and narrow path. When I would have gone astray, she prayed earnestly and often for me. I thank God for my mother. It was because of her that I avoided lots of trouble in my early years. I never smoked a cigarette in my life. Mommy told me, "If I ever catch you with a cigarette, I'm gonna make you eat it." And I couldn't help thinking, "Did she mean lit or unlit?" Either way, I wasn't willing to chance it…no cigarettes for me.

I knew she wanted the best for me, but that did not mean I preferred the strict discipline and endless training. I somehow could not reconcile how the belt, the "switch," or whatever instrument of refinement used to enhance my character resembled anything remotely close to love. Yet, when I look at my life now, I'm so thankful for the things she taught me, even with the rod of correction. I'm thankful *now* but while I was undergoing training in my parents' boot camp (I haven't said very much about it, but Dad was very much a part of the process as well), I thought I would be much better off on my own. I believed I would be happier in a place where no one could tell me what to do, where to go, or how to behave. Have you ever felt like that?

Perhaps it's just me, but I was a pretty strong-willed little fellow. I was convinced that I knew what was best for me. If I could just get everybody else to do what I said, then everything would flow much more smoothly. Then one day, I had an epiphany! The idea was *so* clever, I was sure it would solve all my problems. I, Lawrence Powell, was running away! I'd show Mommy who was boss.

Confidently, I planted my feet and prepared to make my official announcement. You should've seen me. I was about to set some things in order at the Powell estate. I opened my mouth and blurted out, "I'm running away!" Now in my mind, I imagined that Mommy's knees would buckle and she would fall down before me crying and pleading with me, "Lawrence, don't go! Please don't go!" But…something went terribly wrong. Instead, she got a suitcase, packed some of my clothes, picked up the phone, and called someone to come and get me. I was thinking, "Wait a minute…Hello? Is this thing on? Can I get some more volume on my mic? Didn't I just say I'm leaving?" And I…well, I stood there bewildered and in shock, because she didn't seem at all affected by the prospect of losing her dear little boy.

By this time my head was spinning, and I was saying to myself, "I...I can't believe this woman is putting me out of my house! I'm just a helpless little boy! Where will I go? What will I eat? Where will I sleep? What have I done?" My plan had backfired like Elmer Fudd's shotgun.

Then the reality of the situation hit me like a ton of bricks and the idea of being on my own quickly lost its allure. I dropped the macho act and started pleading for mercy. That's what I did. It wasn't supposed to happen like that. Now *I* was the one begging for me not to go, as I hurriedly attempted to put my things back into my dresser drawers. My genius plan went bust. And what's worse, I didn't learn until much later, she had not even really called anyone. I got played like a fiddle, but boy did she teach me a lesson—a very valuable one.

I discovered that night, antics and manipulation were not going to change anything. I had to learn the value of submitting to some much-needed discipline. Through the years, I was beaten with many stripes. I was wounded for my transgressions. I was bruised for my iniquities. Before I ever knew the power of the Holy Spirit, the belt was my keeper! In the days we are living in, some people don't believe in spanking. They worry about their children calling the Child Abuse Hotline, but not in my mother's house. Mommy made it very clear that a phone call to DYFS, New Jersey's Division of Youth and Family Services, would be a complete and utter waste of time. God had not given her the spirit of fear. She would confidently and constantly say, "I wish they would come to *my* house. They'll get a beatin' too!"

I cannot say that I enjoyed her methods of correction and painful chastisement, but I can say *it was good for me that I was afflicted.* Even though I didn't like it, I needed it. By now, you may be wondering if I was a bad child. Well, of course I don't see it that way. I like to think that I was a young, burgeoning leader. I was just a little ahead of my season. I didn't quite know how to properly channel my strong leadership capabilities. I was a young Joseph of sorts, who was often misunderstood by his family. Maybe I was a little mischievous on occasion and rebellious at times, but I can say this much, Mommy did a fine job keeping me on track.

Similarly, God does whatever is necessary to help us reach our full potential. He chastises and corrects us when we need it. His purpose is to get us into alignment to prepare us for our future. The next time you think about running away from the heat of refinement and the discomfort of staunch discipline, take a moment to think about the alternative—a purposeless life. Then ask yourself, "Is my comfort more important than my destiny?" If you cannot respond affirmatively to that question, then be still and take the heat.

❧ TAKE A GOOD LOOK AT YOURSELF ❧

When is the last time you took a long, hard, honest look at yourself in the light of God's Word? How did you measure up? I believe we have to engage in regularly scheduled check-ups. "Examine yourselves *as to* whether you are in the faith" (2 Corinthians 13:5 NKJV). Each day presents a new opportunity to lay your issues bare before God and ask Him to unveil what is truly beneath the mask. If you have not done it lately, how many moments will you let pass before you allow God to reveal those areas in you that need work?

You have an open invitation to meet the Father in prayer. Your moment for a visitation from Him has not expired. Draw near to Him with a sincere heart. He's waiting patiently. You can meet Him anywhere. It doesn't have to happen while seated on a padded pew in the sanctuary of a local church. You may be driving in your vehicle or kneeling at your bedside. You might even be in the hospital, but wherever you are, God wants to commune with you. The promise is still true today, "Draw near to God and He will draw near to you" (James 4:8a NKJV).

God wants you to take a good look at yourself, so you can uncover your identity—the good, the bad, and the ugly. You're at a crossroads in your life. Either you can pretend to have it all together, or finally fess up and tell God, "It's not my mother, not my father, but it's me, oh Lord, standing in the need of prayer."

Have you ever noticed that when you sincerely bask in His holy presence, He inevitably uncovers your weaknesses, mess-ups, and deep secrets? It's at this point that you become keenly aware of your vulnerability before Him. You are forced to deal with your humanity. That's what happened to the prophet Isaiah one day when he was in the temple. He experienced an unmistakable manifestation of God's power. He saw the Lord high and lifted up and responded by saying, "Woe is me, for I am undone! Because I am a man of unclean lips, and I dwell in the midst of a people of unclean lips; For my eyes have seen the King, the LORD of hosts" (Isaiah 6:5 NKJV). When you see God clearly, you are bound to see yourself clearly also.

Are you humble enough to admit that there are areas in you that yet need to be fixed? If you ignore your own fallibility and humanness, you'll be easily deceived by Satan, who desires to sift you as wheat. "But we are all as an unclean thing, and all our righteousnesses are as filthy rags" (Isaiah 64:6a KJV). Never

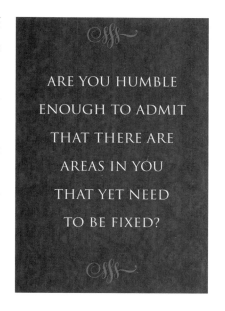

ARE YOU HUMBLE ENOUGH TO ADMIT THAT THERE ARE AREAS IN YOU THAT YET NEED TO BE FIXED?

forget that self-righteousness is unrighteousness. Underneath that facade of false piety is dross that needs to be removed.

It is necessary to take the heat and let God rid you of harmful elements that contaminate your character. Otherwise, you will lead a double life and the duality of your nature will catch up to you quickly. At some point someone is bound to do or say something that triggers the part of you that you have worked so hard to conceal. And trust me when I say, Satan knows just how to push your buttons. If you have some unrefined areas in your life which you've chosen to ignore, be prepared. That dross will come floating to the surface at the most inopportune time.

Don't find yourself with the "other you" being revealed and "Mr. Hyde," coming out of hiding for everyone to see. Don't be that person who's usually quiet, sensitive, and level-headed who turns into the Incredible Hulk...and *nobody likes you when you're angry!* That's why you have to take a good look at yourself and deal with your issues. You can never predict what will happen in the course of a day. I can remember several years ago being seriously slighted and mistreated by someone. I was shocked by their behavior and baffled by the offense against me. Thankfully, on this particular occasion, I was able to maintain my composure.

Admittedly, there have been plenty of times I lost my cool. This time, despite the injustice, I can remember feeling really good about my attitude. I was thinking, "I must *really* be saved." Even so, I discussed the ordeal with a friend and colleague. He so graciously offered a listening ear and a witty response. He was glad to hear of my victory in Jesus and jokingly said, "Man...you're better than me. If that were me, I would've cussed 'em out first and asked for forgiveness later!" At least I *think* he was joking.

If you are in agreement with that opinion, lay your hand on your head and say, "Come out Satan! I rebuke you right now in Jesus name." Say out loud, "I will *not* be a cussin' saint!" And if, by chance, you have a problem bridling your tongue then the altar at your local church is waiting for you. In this way, I am unapologetically old school. Profanity and cussing is a part of the old man, a manner in which we lived apart from Christ. "*Let* your speech always *be* with grace, seasoned with salt, that you may know how you ought to answer each one" (Colossians 4:6 NKJV).

I know the Bible tells us, "But no man can tame the tongue. *It is* an unruly evil, full of deadly poison" (James 3:8 NKJV). But that is not a license to use profanity. If you have a problem with your mouth, whether it's cussing, fussing, gossiping, or backbiting; it's not really a *mouth problem*. Instead, it's a *heart problem*. "Keep your heart with all diligence, For out of it *spring* the issues of life" (Proverbs 4:23 NKJV). Jesus said, "For out of the abundance of the heart the mouth speaks" (Matthew 12:34b NKJV). When your heart is pure, everything that flows from your mouth should also be pure. Foul language cannot "slip out" of you, if it is not in your heart to begin with.

I'm not suggesting anyone is perfect. We all end up having to apologize at some point. Still, we must strive for perfection or better stated, maturity. The Bible says, "For we all stumble in many things. If anyone does not stumble in word, he *is* a perfect man" (James 3:2a NKJV). Obviously, none of us is flawless. I just want you to see that you must allow God to work on your inner man, so that what comes out of you will bring glory to Him, rather than shame.

No, you need not rush to the bathroom to wash your mouth out with soap. External cleansing won't help, when you need internal purging. No amount of behavior modification can substitute for genuine inward transformation. Change begins within and then manifests on the outside. Not the other way around.

This is the principle Jesus taught the Pharisees when they asked Him, "Why walk not thy disciples according to the tradition of the elders, but eat bread with unwashed hands?" (Mark 7:5). In response to this question, He explained to them that an individual's failure to observe certain external religious rituals did not make them unclean. Rather, defilement is the direct result of an unregenerate heart.

Jesus told them, "For from within, out of the heart of men, proceed evil thoughts, adulteries, fornications, murders, Thefts, covetousness, wickedness, deceit, lasciviousness, an evil eye, blasphemy, pride, foolishness: All these evil things come from within, and defile the man" (Mark 7:21-23 NKJV). God is not focused on outward symbols of devoutness; He wants a pure heart. "The refining pot is for silver and the furnace for gold, but the LORD tests the hearts" (Proverbs 17:3 NKJV). Jesus said, "Blessed are the pure in heart: for they shall see God" (Matthew 5:8 KJV). Sin originates in the heart and shows up in your actions. Don't seek God for a change in behavior, ask Him for a change of heart.

"To try to change outward attitudes and behaviors does very little good in the long run if we fail to examine the basic paradigms from which those attitudes and behaviors flow." (Stephen Covey, The Seven Habits of Highly Effective People; New York; Simon & Schuster, 1990, p. 28). I admonish you to get in God's presence, so He can unveil your issues.

I'm sure King David did not know how many impurities were inside of him, until Satan found his trigger. Her name was Bathsheba. He was up on the rooftop when he caught a glimpse of her while she was bathing. What did he do? He kept on looking. Rather than resist the temptation, he committed adultery with her, impregnated her, and had her husband, Uriah, killed to cover up the mess he made (2 Samuel 11).

I told you earlier, no one is perfect. We sometimes make dreadful mistakes. It is crucial to *submit yourself to God. Fast and pray. Study His Word. Get lost in worship, and examine yourself.* So, when the enemy tries to tempt and trap you, you will be equipped to resist him by the power of the Holy Spirit. "Surely He shall deliver you from the snare of the fowler" (Psalm 91:3 NKJV). It takes God to keep you in alignment. Anytime you lose sight of that fact, you're on a sure path that leads to sin. "Therefore let him who thinks he stands take heed lest he fall" (1 Corinthians 10:12 NKJV).

You may not believe you will ever mess up as badly as David did. I'm sure he never imagined he would commit such heinous acts either. After all, he truly loved God. David was an anointed worship leader, psalmist, and musician. Furthermore, he was God's choice to succeed Saul as King of all Israel. He was a real man after God's heart (Acts 13:22). Yet, even he was in need of refinement.

God used the Prophet Nathan to confront David about the horrible acts he committed, by telling him the following story:

> There were two men in a certain town, one rich and the other poor. The rich man had a very large number of sheep and cattle, but the poor man had nothing except one little ewe lamb he had bought. He raised it, and it grew up with him and his children. It shared his food, drank from his cup and even slept in his arms. It was like a daughter to him.
>
> Now a traveler came to the rich man, but the rich man refrained from taking one of his own sheep or cattle to prepare a meal for the traveler who had come to him. Instead, he took the ewe lamb that belonged to the poor man and prepared it for the one who had come to him.

David burned with anger against the man and said to Nathan, "As surely as the LORD lives, the man who did this deserves to die! He must pay for that lamb four times over, because he did such a thing and had no pity."

Then Nathan said to David, "You are the man!" (2 Samuel 12:1-7 NIV)

Now, I'm sure David did not expect to hear that the antagonistic rich man in the story was, in fact, him! God called him on the carpet. He was forced to look at his own moral depravity and deal with the ugliness inside him. Once David came to grips with what was really going on, he did not make any excuses. He did not justify his wrongdoing, rather, he fervently cried out to God for forgiveness and cleansing.

He said, "Purge me with hyssop, and I shall be clean; Wash me, and I shall be whiter than snow" (Psalm 51:7 NKJV). Hyssop was a plant used for the purposes of purification and ritual acts of cleansing (Leviticus 14:4; Numbers 19:6). As a matter of fact, hyssop was also used during the time of the seventh plague in the land of Egypt when the Angel of Death was smiting the firstborn son in every household. The Israelites dipped the hyssop plant in the blood of a sacrificial lamb and sprinkled it over their doorways, so death would not come near their houses (Exodus 12:22).

This time, David needed God to blot out *his* transgressions, cleanse him from all his iniquities and restore him back to his rightful place. Fortunately, he swallowed his pride and stopped masquerading. He was finally ready for God to refine his design and make him "whiter than snow." The truth emerges clearly from the request of David that the stain and reproach of sin could only be removed by the fuller's soap. Why the fuller?

A fuller was a professional tradesman who specialized in whitening garments. No one could get a piece of fabric quite as clean as the fuller could, no matter how soiled, dirty, or stained. The combination of his special soap and unique method penetrated the fibers of the garment, removing every trace of filth and grime. Generally, he would use ashes from certain plants that contained alkaline as the primary cleansing agent. He also rubbed the garment together using putrid urine and chalk, much the way we use bleach to aid in the whitening process. Can you imagine the stench? Aside from wetting the garment, he also stomped it with his feet and beat it with rods to get it good and white.

The procedure was by no means delicate. The substances used to cleanse the garment were odorously offensive. However, no one could dispute the effectiveness of the fuller's process. You may not prefer God's method. Yet, when it is all said and done, you won't doubt that He has made an awesome difference in your life.

STAY IN THE ❧ CENTER OF ❧ HIS WHEEL

It's amazing to see all of the extraordinary creations of pottery that began as lumps of clay. Intriguingly, there

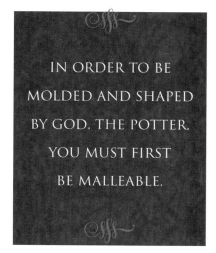

IN ORDER TO BE MOLDED AND SHAPED BY GOD, THE POTTER, YOU MUST FIRST BE MALLEABLE.

are countless different designs. Each and every one reflects the unique vision of the potter who molded it. You must know that God has a specific design and purpose just for you. In order to be molded and shaped by God, the Potter, you must first be malleable. In other words, you have to completely give over to the Master's hands.

Have you ever sat down to drink a hot beverage from an authentic pottery teacup? Have you ever stopped to think about the fact that it began as a simple lump of clay? It had no shape, no design, and no purpose, until it was placed on a spinning wheel, and molded by the capable hands of a skilled potter. Like the teacup, God wants to mold you into a vessel of honor, beauty, and purpose. But you must be still and let Him refine your design.

In the art of pottery making, it is crucial for the clay to remain in the center of the spinning wheel so that it can be properly shaped and sculpted. Similarly, in your walk with God, you, too, must stay in the center of His will in order for Him to fashion you into something more beautiful than you could have ever imagined. If at anytime the clay resists the molding of the potter, it can very easily end up marred, just like the clay in the book of Jeremiah. The clay represents rebellious Israel, the chosen people of God.

"This is the word that came to Jeremiah from the LORD: 'Go down to the potter's house, and there I will give you my message.' So I went down to the potter's house, and I saw him working at the wheel. But the pot he was shaping from the clay was marred in his hands; so the potter formed it into another pot, shaping it as seemed best to him" (Jeremiah 18:1-4 NIV).

Do you see what happened to the unyielding clay? It was ruined in the potter's hands, so he molded it into something else. God was making a point to Jeremiah. He wanted Jeremiah to let the children of Israel know, if they were obedient, they would experience His favor and blessings. If they were disobedient, however, they would not flourish into all He desired them to be. He wanted so much to do great and awesome things for His chosen people, but they had to first surrender to Him. They needed to stay in the center of His wheel.

The same applies to both you and me. Obedience is a must if we expect God to pour out abundant blessings upon us and equip us to fulfill our purpose. Nevertheless, even when we fall short, God is merciful. He will not release us from His providential care. He loves us far too much to cast us aside. "All that the Father gives Me will come to Me, and the one who comes to Me I will by no means cast out" (John 6:37 NKJV). Rather than throw us away, the loving Potter takes that which is broken, and puts it back together again, in a way that pleases Him.

Friend, even when our lives are marred by sin, mistakes, and regrets, God extends His abundant grace to us. Thankfully, He gives us what no one else can. That is the chance to begin again. As we yield to Him, He will refine our design. "But in a great house there are not only vessels of gold and silver, but also of wood and clay, some for honor and some for dishonor. Therefore if anyone cleanses himself from the latter, he will be a vessel for honor, sanctified and useful for the Master, prepared for every good work" (2 Timothy 2:20-21 NKJV).

You may not know exactly what He is molding you into, but continue to remain yielded and still. Although each piece of the puzzle is not in place, you have to trust that God knows what He is doing. "Woe to him who strives with his Maker! Let the potsherd strive with the potsherds of the earth! Shall the clay say to him who forms it, 'What are you making?' Or shall your handiwork *say*, 'He has no hands'?" (Isaiah 45:9 NKJV).

The Prophet Isaiah was making the point that it is God's prerogative to mold you into whatever He desires you to be. Your job is to let Him do the designing. Isaiah paints an image of how absurd it would be for a lump of clay to say to the potter, "Hey! What are you doing with me? What are you shaping me into? When are you going to let me off this wheel? Why are you smothering me and crushing me with your hands? Let me go free!"

It is easy to see how ridiculous that notion is. Why then, do we strive with God, our Creator? Do we really think we have the right to advise Him about what He should do, how He should do it, and how long we should be subjected to His process? "For we are His workmanship, created in Christ Jesus for good works, which God prepared beforehand that we should walk in them" (Ephesians 2:10 NKJV).

He already knows the path that you must take and He has created the blueprints for your life. In order for Him to mold you according to His design, you have to submit. If you remain in His capable hands, He will refine your design and mold you into the glorious vessel He has in mind.

CHAPTER 5

KEEP ON KEEPIN' ON

Failure is the Path of Least Persistence

UNKNOWN

Because you are God's chosen, that makes you a prime target for your chief adversary, Satan. He knows that if he can get to you, he can get to God, since you are the apple of His eye (See Zechariah 2:8). This makes you the object of Satan's malevolent intentions. To this end, he repeatedly tries to destroy you through vile attacks of every kind. Nevertheless, you will always overcome by the grace and faithfulness of the Lord.

Have you ever considered why those things that came to kill, steal from, and destroy you in times past, failed? It was because of the preeminent plans of the Father. You must understand that He is a God of purpose. And though opposition may abound, God's desires always prevail in the end. The Lord reigns. He occupies His lofty and majestic throne, commanding in appearance and always awesome in power. No matter how bad things may look, God is still in control. When you are going through an attack of the enemy, you can keep on keepin' on, without wavering.

Persecution will not kill you. Quite the contrary, you will grow stronger having gone through it with the Lord. Have you ever noticed that difficult situations have a way of thickening your skin and toughening you up? That's what adversity does; it serves as the friction needed to sharpen you. You will become wiser, more refined, more discriminating, and more strategic. You won't be easily intimidated and you won't be duped as often by deceptive tactics. In other words, you will grow up if you let God do His thing in the midst of your persecution. And I say if, because, you always have other options like: running away, throwing in the towel, abandoning your purpose, and fading away into oblivion. Only you can decide whether you'll keep on keepin' on, or give up when the pressure is on. It is totally up to you.

Certainly, you can take the easy way out and be a people pleaser. That is, if you've always dreamed of being a puppet. If you don't mind saying what they want you to say, doing what they want you to do, going where they want you to go, and ultimately, being who they want you to be, you'll be a perfect fit. You never again have to worry about thinking for yourself. You can relax and let them do all the thinking for you. Imagine how exciting it will be to let the puppet masters program you to say the same two or three phrases over and over again. Then you can politely wait for them to pull the string in your back, before you speak.

I know that is not the life you've always wanted. It's a ridiculous idea. Perhaps it seems silly, but many people live their lives that way. They do everything in their power to avoid controversy. Consequently, in their quest to placate everyone, they end up abandoning their purpose. Like chameleons, they do whatever is necessary to blend into their surroundings. They become whoever they need to be so they don't step on anyone's toes. People like this rarely, if ever, say what they are really thinking. Anything close to their real opinion might cause entirely too much trouble.

This wouldn't describe you, would it? You aren't incessantly trying to avoid conflict, are you? Let's see, is it common for you to abandon a particular course of action if you're met with too much resistance? Take a good look now and begin dealing with your confrontation issues.

If it just so happens that I've pegged you today and you genuinely struggle in this area, I have the cure.

1. Face opposition head on.
2. Press forward anyway.
3. Repeat steps one and two.

That's really all there is to it. There is no other way to deal with adversity. Possibility thinking won't do it. Positive affirmations won't suffice. Standing in the mirror saying, "I think I can. I think I can. I think I can…" is not going to cut

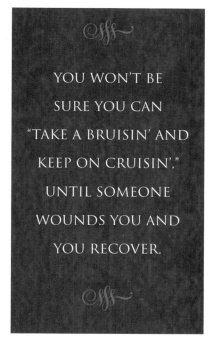

YOU WON'T BE SURE YOU CAN "TAKE A BRUISIN' AND KEEP ON CRUISIN'," UNTIL SOMEONE WOUNDS YOU AND YOU RECOVER.

it. There is simply no substitute for taking some knocks. Trust me, hands-on experience is the way to go. You won't know you can "take a lickin' and keep on tickin'," until you endure an intense attack and still come out a winner. You won't be sure you can "take a bruisin' and keep on cruisin'," until someone wounds you and you recover. Until you press on when you want to quit, you won't know that you can keep on keepin' on, even when times get rough.

Ideally, things would go smoothly, everyone would smile, hold hands, and sing Kumbaya. But the reality is, you will lose friends and gain enemies along the way. Will it be hard sometimes? Yes. Will people turn on you? Absolutely. Will you be misunderstood often? Sure will. But here's your consolation: God will never leave you alone. Your Heavenly Father will be there to comfort and protect you. He will, undoubtedly, strengthen and equip you for the road ahead. With this in mind, you can confidently rely on His sustaining power. The more you trust Him, the sooner you will be able to join the ranks of great men and women of God who have dared to do awesome things for the Kingdom.

In August of 2006, I had the great privilege of meeting one such man in the person of Dr. Oral Roberts, the renowned healing evangelist and founder of Oral Roberts University. I visited him in his home in California. I must say, it was by far, one of the most inspirational experiences of my life. While sitting there in the presence of a man who has performed such formidable and notable things for the Kingdom of God, I was truly humbled.

I settled in, eager to hear what Dr. Roberts had to say. Initially, we casually conversed and shared a few laughs. Then, as we moved forward in our discussion, he asked me a question. He said, "What are some of the things you learned as a student at ORU?" I had come that day expecting only to sit and learn from him and when he gave me the floor, I was slightly caught off guard. I thought for a moment. Then I shared with him the most vital thing I learned before graduating.

I did not talk about Greek and Hebrew translations of Scripture. I did not try to impress him with my ability to exegete a text. Nor did I bore him with citations from my favorite Biblical scholars. Instead, I took the opportunity to tell him what I learned from his life that had so profoundly influenced me and my ministry. I said, "I learned from you, how to be like Nehemiah and stay on the wall even in the face of persecution." Certainly Dr. Roberts knows what it means to endure harsh attacks and overcome insurmountable obstacles. He has stood firmly through relentless media onslaughts, violent threats, and even an assassination attempt. During a crusade in the 1940's, a man fired a shot at him, missing only by a narrow margin. Yet, Dr. Roberts did not give up the good fight of faith.

Just as all great men and women have, we too will face adversity. We will not all experience the same degree of persecution, but we each must go through it on some level. Be prepared. By no means can you accomplish anything of significance without facing and overcoming opposition.

If you endure, God's glory will shine through you with all the brilliance of a scintillating star. He will elevate you to levels of victory you can't even imagine. As you stand firmly rooted in Him and keep on keepin' on, you will experience the glorious elation of hard-fought victory. Don't give up. Be a valiant and vigorous soldier for the Lord. Follow the instructions that Paul gave to Timothy, "You therefore must endure hardship as a good soldier of Jesus Christ" (2 Timothy 2:3 NKJV).

❧ KNOW WHO YOU ARE FIGHTING ❧

Before you can successfully win a battle, you must know who you're fighting against. Sadly, people inadvertently commit egregious acts against their brothers and sisters in Christ, when the real culprit is Satan. I am not insinuating that people will not commit persecutory acts against you. Don't be naïve. They do it all the time. "Where do wars and fights *come*from among you? Do *they*not *come*from your *desires for* pleasure that war in your members? You lust and do not have. You murder and covet and cannot obtain. You fight and war" (James 4:1-2 NKJV). The Bible is clear on this point; there are treacherous people in the world.

Still, there is a spiritual battle raging that goes much deeper than what we see. If we neglect that fact, we will fight and plot against each other. All the while, our real enemy will run free, stirring up trouble in the Body of Christ.

There is a story of two brothers, the eldest whose name was John and the youngest whose name was James. The two lived on adjoining farms. One day they got into a conflict. For 40 years, they had been farming side by side, sharing machinery, trading labor and goods, without a single quarrel. It all began with a small misunderstanding. Gradually, it grew into a major difference. Finally, it exploded into an exchange of bitter words followed by weeks of silence.

One morning out of the blue, there was a knock on John's door. He opened it, to find a man with a carpenter's toolbox. Oddly, he had never seen this man in the neighborhood, but he seemed harmless enough. John asked, "What is it?"

The man said, "Hello sir, I'm looking for a few days work. If you have any small jobs here and there, would you consider hiring me?"

Quite honestly, John wasn't thinking of bringing on any extra help at that time, but then, he got a bright idea. Suddenly, a broad smile came across the older brother's face and he said, "Ah yes, I know just the thing…I have the perfect job for you!"

The strange carpenter stood there with his toolbox, waiting to hear what it was. Then John pointed his finger and said, "Look across the creek. Do you see that farm over there?" The carpenter swung his head around quickly, looked and said, "Oh sure, I see it. What of it?"

John said, "That's my neighbor's farm. Actually, it belongs to my younger brother. Anyhow, last week, there was only a meadow between us."

"That's odd," said the carpenter, "There's a creek full of water there now. I don't understand. How did that happen?"

The older brother rolled his eyes in the air and said, "I couldn't believe it when he did it but, he took his bulldozer, knocked down the levee, and that's how the creek got between us. I think he did it to spite me. I bet you I'll show him."

The carpenter grimaced a little and said, "I don't see what all this has to do with the job you want me to do for you, sir." The older brother laughed heartily, "I'm sorry, I got caught up there for a moment." He gathered himself and pointed again, "Do you see that pile of lumber by the barn?"

"Yes," said the carpenter.

"Well, I want you to build me a fence, an 8-foot fence, so I won't ever have to look at James or his farm anymore. Now, I'll see what he thinks about that." The older brother seemed pleased by the idea. The carpenter said, "I think I understand the situation and what you want me to do. Will you show me where the nails are and the post-hole digger, so I'll be able to do a job that pleases you?"

The older brother said, "I like your attitude. I think you'll do just fine around here." After he got the carpenter all settled, he had to go into town for some supplies. He told his new worker that he would be gone for the rest of the day.

All that day, the carpenter worked very hard, measuring, sawing, and nailing. Finally, at about sunset when older brother returned home, the carpenter had just finished his job. The older brother stopped and stared...speechless. His eyes opened wide and his jaw dropped.

There was no 8-foot fence in sight. The carpenter had not done what he asked.

Instead, he had built a huge bridge…and the bridge spanned from the older brother's side of the creek to the younger brother's side! The bridge was a fine spectacle, complete with handrails and all. While John stood in awe, James was running across, his hand outstretched.

"I'm so ashamed," said the older brother.

Finally, the two brothers met in the middle of the bridge, embraced, and apologized for being so ridiculous. They turned just in time to see the strange carpenter hoisting his toolbox onto his shoulder.

"No, wait!" John called after him. "Please stay for a few days. I've got a bunch of other projects for you."

"I'd love to stay," the carpenter said, "but, I have many more bridges to build."

If we are not careful, we too, will be building walls when we should be building bridges. We need each other and Satan hates nothing more than to see God's people unified. He loves to see schisms, factions, and cliques in the church. This is not what God wants. "That there should be no schism in the body, but that the members should have the same care for one another" (1 Corinthians 12:25 NKJV). Satan knows as long as we are persecuting and fighting against each other, we'll be ineffective in the Kingdom of God. "If a kingdom is divided against itself, that kingdom cannot stand" (Mark 3:24 NKJV).

At some point, we have to shake ourselves and ask, "Have we forgotten who we're fighting against? Have we been so busy accusing one another that we've overlooked the 'accuser of our brethren'?"

(See Revelation 12:10.) While forwarding our own selfish agendas, we end up attacking, rather than assisting; hurting, rather than helping; criticizing, rather than edifying (Ephesians 4:16).

Let us be careful not to get off course and end up fighting the wrong war, as well as the wrong adversary. "For we do not wrestle against flesh and blood, but against principalities, against powers, against the rulers of the darkness of this age, against spiritual hosts of wickedness in the heavenly places" (Ephesians 6:12 NKJV). The battle is spiritual, but it manifests in the natural. That's why you have to be ever so careful. Many times, people are under Satan's influence and he uses them to hinder your calling.

SATAN AND ALL OF HIS DEMONS ARE IN FACT SPIRITS, WORKING THROUGH OTHER PEOPLE TO GET TO YOU.

It's a misconception to think that the devil is an ugly, ghoulish creature, lurking in the shadows, dressed in a red caped suit, with horns on his head, cleft feet, a pointed tail, and pitchfork in his hand. Satan and all of his demons are in fact spirits, working through other people to get to you. It's true; your chief adversary inhabits some of the very people you encounter on a daily basis. In light of this fact, you need to be on guard.

If you are not careful, you will not be balanced in your approach to human relationships. Although God calls us to love one another, don't be foolish. You must be wise and watchful. Jesus said, "Behold, I send you out as sheep in the midst of wolves. Therefore be wise as serpents and harmless as doves. But beware of men, for they will deliver you up to councils and scourge you in their synagogues" (Matthew 10:16-17 NKJV). Jesus was teaching the disciples how to have good sense. He did not want them to be instigators, but he also did not want them to be ignorant. He let them know that there would be some who would scandalize their names, set them up, and sell them down the river.

Have you ever heard people say, "Learn to sleep with one eye open?" That simply means, don't ever let your guard all the way down. That is dangerous. If you do, you could get caught out there. Have you ever had a friend or a close family member turn against you for no apparent reason? If so, you can attest to the fact that the devil orchestrates and instigates confrontations to advance his destructive plans. Sometimes he works through a co-worker, who smiles in your face and runs your name in the ground behind your back. At other times he uses your so-called best friend, who lends a listening ear one night and puts all your business in the street the following day.

Come on back. Don't go drifting down memory lane on me. I'm not sharing those examples to get you riled up. Rather, I'm trying to get you to see the bigger picture. There is always a spirit operating behind every attack. Until you understand this, you'll continually be sidetracked by trivial things. The devil is shameless. He'll use anyone who is open, willing, and available, particularly those closest to you.

Certain events in the life of King David perfectly demonstrate how friends and loved ones can be used to cause confusion in your life. Unfortunately, David was the cause of much of his own trouble.

After he committed adultery with Bathsheba, God pronounced judgment on his household. Subsequently, this set off a series of unfortunate incidents and one in particular.

David's son, Absalom, orchestrated a coup against his own father, in an effort to steal the throne. In 2 Samuel 15, Absalom successfully turned many people against David. Even his trusted counselor, Ahithophel, sided with Absalom to carry out his sinister plan. As you can imagine, David was in torment over the whole incident and expressed his feelings in Psalm 55:12-13. He said, "For *it is* not an enemy *who* reproaches me; Then I could bear *it*. Nor *is*

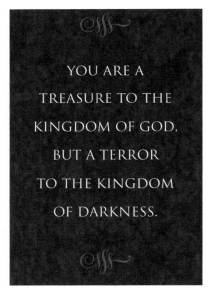

YOU ARE A TREASURE TO THE KINGDOM OF GOD, BUT A TERROR TO THE KINGDOM OF DARKNESS.

it one *who* hates me who has exalted *himself* against me; Then I could hide from him. But *it was* you, a man my equal, My companion and my acquaintance" (NKJV).

Can you sense the pain and anguish he feels as a result of being betrayed? Keep living long enough and you may find that people will stab you in the back, then show up regularly to make sure the knife is still in place. No one is exempt. We all, at some point, will be wounded at the hand of someone we love. In these moments, be careful not to lose your focus. Remind yourself that Satan does not want you to make an impact in the world. He hates everything you stand for. When you walk in your calling, you make his job more difficult. You are a treasure to the Kingdom of God, but a terror to the kingdom of darkness. Stay alert; you never know who he will use.

Satan even utilized Jesus' disciples. As is commonly the case, they didn't even realize it. It happened one day while Jesus was preparing them for His death and resurrection.

> From that time Jesus began to show His disciples that He must go to Jerusalem, and suffer many things from the elders and chief priests and scribes, and be killed, and be raised the third day. Then Peter took Him aside and began to rebuke Him, saying "Far be it from You, Lord; this shall not happen to You!" But He turned and said to Peter "Get behind Me, Satan! You are an offense to Me, for you are not mindful of the things of God, but the things of men." (Matthew 16:21-23 NKJV)

Ponder what happened for a moment. Can you imagine the expression on Peter's face when Jesus looked at him squarely in the eye and said, "Get behind me Satan?" I'm sure he felt a little confused, hurt, and surprised by his Master's rebuttal. Surely, he meant well. Peter was only trying to protect Jesus from harm. Obviously, he didn't have a full revelation of the purpose for which Christ had to die. So, why would Jesus say that to him? Wasn't that a little harsh? After all, Peter was one of Jesus' most avid supporters.

If you are asking that question, you are missing the whole point. Jesus was not talking to him, not at all. He was, in truth, addressing the spirit at work in Peter. Sometimes, even the most well-intentioned people are being employed by the devil as influences specially designed to keep you off track, off focus, and off the path that leads to your purpose. Satan knew full well that Jesus came to earth to die on the cross for the sins of the world to reconcile humankind back to God. Needless to say, Christ's agenda was diametrically opposed to that of Satan's.

Bearing that in mind, it's no surprise that the devil would use Peter to vehemently oppose Jesus' death. This was a direct assault on His life's purpose. That is why Jesus was always on guard. "Be sober, be vigilant; because your adversary the devil walks about like a roaring lion, seeking whom he may devour" (1 Peter 5:8 NKJV). He knew the forces of darkness were working tirelessly to undermine His Heavenly mission.

Knowing this, it behooves each of us to guard our hearts and seek God for direction. He will reveal the plans of the enemy. That way, we won't waste our time fighting each other, instead of our real enemy, Satan.

❧ DON'T BE FOOLED BY NUMBERS ❧

You need not walk around timid and intimidated. There is nothing that anyone can do to hinder the good plans God has already laid out for you. That does not mean, however, you won't sometimes have to go through intense attacks. There's no escaping that. There will be moments when you feel vulnerable and alone. You'll feel outnumbered, but don't be fooled by numbers. You have God on your side.

Still, you may wonder if God sees or cares about what's happening. Not only does He see, but He's also present with you. Consider what the Prophet Elijah was going through when he was on the run from Jezebel, the infamously wicked wife of King Ahab (1 Kings 19). Not only was she immoral, but Ahab was also notoriously corrupt.

Together, this destructive duo wreaked havoc on the prophets of God and led the nation of Israel into the worship of Baal. This did not bode well for Elijah's mission. He was sent by God to turn the people's hearts back toward righteousness.

Conversely, Jezebel relentlessly slaughtered God's prophets. As a result, they hid in caves. "For so it was, while Jezebel massacred the prophets of the LORD, that Obadiah had taken one hundred prophets and hidden them, fifty to a cave, and had fed them with bread and water" (1 Kings 18:4 NKJV). Ironically, Obadiah, Ahab's trusted official, feared God. He helped the men of God stay out of harms way.

The treachery had run amuck in Israel, such that no prophet that feared the Lord was safe. Under this administration, brute force and tyrannical authority was the norm. Elijah, unlike the other prophets, was undaunted by what was going on. He had faith in the God of his salvation. He boldly burst on the scene and immediately requested to see Ahab (18:8).

This was a courageous move on the part of Elijah. Showing up should have meant certain death for him. It was no secret that Ahab hated him. The King's contempt was so strong that he had previously sent bounty hunters all throughout the land, seeking after Elijah (18:10). Finally, when the two met up, the first words out of Ahab's mouth were, "Is that you, O troubler of Israel?" (18:17). It was established from the outset that this was in no way a happy encounter.

Elijah had come for two reasons. First, he sought to expose Baal for the fraud that he was. Second, he longed to prove that the God he served was, in fact, real.

Elijah issued a bold challenge to Ahab. He said, "Now therefore, send and gather all Israel to me on Mount Carmel, the four hundred and fifty prophets of Baal, and the four hundred prophets of Asherah, who eat at Jezebel's table" (18:19). In response to Elijah's audacious request, Ahab rounded everyone up. There was about to be a showdown on Mount Carmel.

Undeniably, Elijah was way outnumbered. In this case, the majority ruled. How big was the gap in the numbers? There were a total of 850 prophets, against one! "...the four hundred and fifty prophets of Baal, and the four hundred prophets of Asherah, who eat at Jezebel's table" (18:19b). But it didn't matter, because Elijah had the Lord on his side.

If you are looking to win a popularity contest, you may be in for a rude awakening. God has not chosen you just so you can have fine cars, clothes, jewelry, houses, land, and a myriad of other material possessions. Though I do believe He will bless you with all those things, they can't be your primary focus. You must be more interested in winning souls to the Kingdom. Remember, people are dying without the Lord.

So many individuals have been duped and led astray by the pervasive immorality in our society. But it's up to you and me to exemplify Christ to a dying world. "You are the light of the world. A city that is set on a hill cannot be hidden. Nor do they light a lamp and put it under a basket, but on a lampstand, and it gives light to all who are in the house. Let your light so shine before men, that they may see your good works and glorify your Father in heaven" (Matthew 5:14-16 NKJV). It's about bringing glory to the Father and denouncing everything that is not like Him. It's about refusing to compromise your convictions, even in the face of unrelenting persecution.

Even when the "Jezebels" and "Ahabs" of the world come out of the woodwork, don't worry. You need not fear the vicious attacks of those opposed to your stance. Don't go hiding in the cave. Don't let the storm of adversity cause you to run for cover. No, stand firmly and declare to this wayward generation that God still requires holiness. They may hate you, but don't quit. As Jesus said, "And you will be hated by all for My name's sake" (Matthew 10:22 NKJV).

DON'T LET THE STORM OF ADVERSITY CAUSE YOU TO RUN FOR COVER.

You have to recognize that the more you do for the Lord, the angrier Satan becomes. When you speak truth, you expose his lies. When you spread love, you diminish hatred. It's no wonder Satan tries so hard to stop you. By living holy, you influence others, thus weakening his control in their lives. And that, my friend, comes at a price. That is why God needs someone willing to take the ridicule and stand anyhow. He wants to know, "Are you the one?" Will you, like

Elijah, love Him more than the things of this world? Will you face persecution for His name's sake?

Can He trust you? Can He count on you not to bow to Baal? He certainly could trust Elijah. On Mount Carmel, all Israel, along with the prophets of Baal and Asherah, watched in awe, as God miraculously displayed His power. In response to Elijah's prayer, God rained down fire from heaven and consumed Elijah's sacrifice. Conversely, the false god Baal never responded to the ridiculous antics of the 850 prophets. This demonstrates that it does not matter how many voices are calling, if there is no god to answer.

The deafening silence of Baal that day caused the people to hear the only true and living God. After witnessing a manifestation of His presence, they were moved to worship. "Now when all the people saw it, they fell on their faces; and they said, 'The LORD, He is God! The LORD, He is God!'" (1 Kings 18:39 NKJV).

As you can imagine, the prophets of Baal had sustained humiliating blows to their faith and pride. But Elijah took things one step further. "And Elijah said to them, 'Seize the prophets of Baal! Do not let one of them escape!' So they seized them; and Elijah brought them down to the Brook of Kishon and executed them there" (18:40 NKJV). The disparity in the numbers didn't matter so much then, did it? What the prophets of God had endured at the hands of Jezebel and her cohorts turned back on the false prophets. As the saying goes, "the chickens had come home to roost." Word got back to Jezebel that Elijah had slaughtered 450 prophets of Baal with the sword (1 Kings 18:40).

From that very moment, Jezebel made it her personal mission to get revenge. "Then Jezebel sent a messenger to Elijah, saying, 'So let the gods do to me, and more also, if I do not make your life as the life of one of them by tomorrow about this time'" (1 Kings 19:2 NKJV). In a nutshell she said, "By this time tomorrow, I'm going to kill you." Given the chance, she would have made good on her word.

But Elijah escaped before she had the opportunity. "And when he saw *that,* he arose and ran for his life, and went to Beersheba, which *belongs* to Judah, and left his servant there" (1 Kings 19:3 NKJV). How overwhelmed must he have felt? He was alone and on the run. He was the only prophet who had taken a stand for God; all the others were hiding out. Besides, it seemed that everyone was serving Baal. In reality, this wasn't the case. God told Elijah, "Yet I have reserved seven thousand in Israel, all whose knees have not bowed to Baal, and every mouth that has not kissed him" (1 Kings 19:18 NKJV).

Even so, Elijah felt desolate. Why should he continue proclaiming the things of God, if no one was going to listen? How could he, alone, convert a whole nation? "And he prayed that he might die, and said, 'It is enough! Now, LORD, take my life, for I *am* no better than my fathers!'" (1 Kings 19:4 NKJV).

God, however, wasn't going to take his life, nor would he allow anyone else to do so. Instead, He sent an angel to feed Elijah, to preserve and sustain him while he remained in the wilderness. By the supernatural power of God, he survived off of just two meals without eating anything else for forty days and nights (1 Kings 19:5–8). Even when he reemerged on the scene, God protected him and thwarted the plans of his enemies. As a matter of fact, Elijah would never taste death. He remained on the earth until he miraculously ascended into heaven (2 Kings 2). Ahab and Jezebel, on the other hand, both died very violently (1 Kings 22:29-39; 2 Kings 9:30-37). Just as He did for Elijah, God will always deliver you. He's got your back!

We see from this account, there will be times when it seems like your enemy is prevailing. Those who persecute you will appear to have the advantage, but remember, looks can be very deceiving. Don't ever forget, even when your enemies are more numerous than you, the upper-hand is still yours. In 2 Kings 6, the King of Syria waged war against Israel. King Ben-Hadad would learn quickly that, "the more," doesn't always mean, "the merrier," not when you factor God into the equation.

The problem arose for the Syrians because there was a seer in Israel's camp. God consistently revealed the plans of King Ben-Hadad and his army to Elisha. Each time Elisha would disclose to the King of Israel the exact strategies of their enemies. Much to King Ben-Hadad's consternation, their plans would always be foiled. Quite naturally, he suspected that an internal spy was leaking confidential information. In a sense, he was right.

> Therefore the heart of the king of Syria was greatly troubled by this thing; and he called his servants and said to them, "Will you not show me which of us is for the king of Israel?" And one of his servants said, "None, my lord, O king; but Elisha, the prophet who *is* in Israel, tells the king of Israel the words that you speak

in your bedroom." So he said, "Go and see where he *is*, that I may send and get him." And it was told him, saying, "Surely he is in Dothan." (2 Kings 6:11-13 NKJV)

Once the King knew the identity and location of the culprit, he sent his army out after Elisha. The very next morning, their camp was surrounded. Most people would have responded much like Elisha's servant, Gehazi, who didn't quite know what to do in this situation. He became fearful because of what things looked like. Even though Elisha was looking at the same set of circumstances, he had a completely different response. "So he answered, 'Do not fear, for those who are with us are more than those who are with them'" (2 Kings 6:16 NKJV).

Gehazi must have been wondering whether Elisha was blind. Did he not see all of these horses, chariots, and soldiers, waiting to pummel them? His servant didn't understand that Elisha was not viewing the circumstance through natural eyes; rather, he had the ability to see the unseen.

Most assuredly, on the surface, the situation looked bleak. But Elisha knew something no one else did at the time. Though undetectable to the natural eye, there was a spiritual army that far outnumbered the enemy forces. It does not matter how fast your opposition is closing in on you. The Lord is with you and your enemy will not win. It does not matter that people are out to get you. You are coming out on top. You don't have to worry about who is against you, when you know Who is for you. "And Elisha prayed, and said, 'LORD, I pray, open his eyes that he may see.' Then the LORD opened the eyes of the young man, and he saw. And behold, the mountain *was* full of horses and chariots of fire all around Elisha" (2 Kings 6:17 NKJV).

Once you realize that angels are encamped all around you then, you won't worry so much about your pursuers. They cannot hurt you anyway. They may try, but it won't work. God already has an ambush waiting for them. Let them come. Let them instigate. Let them stir up trouble. Then, let God be God. "Let God arise, Let His enemies be scattered; Let those also who hate Him flee before Him. As smoke is driven away, so drive *them* away; As wax melts before the fire, *So* let the wicked perish at the presence of God" (Psalm 68:1, 2 NKJV).

Just as quickly as they converged, they will be scattered. "The LORD will cause your enemies who rise against you to be defeated before your face; they shall come out against you one way and flee before you seven ways" (Deuteronomy 28:7 NKJV). That means their plans will be completely torn up. All the mess they have been plotting, in an instant, will fall to the ground. God is never caught off guard by the ploys of the wicked. And as long as you listen to His voice, neither will you.

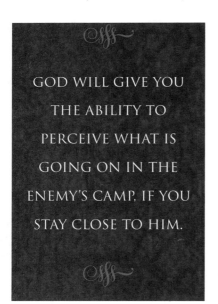

GOD WILL GIVE YOU THE ABILITY TO PERCEIVE WHAT IS GOING ON IN THE ENEMY'S CAMP, IF YOU STAY CLOSE TO HIM.

God will give you the ability to perceive what is going on in the enemy's camp, if you stay close to Him. Spiritual discernment is not something that stopped with Elisha. God still reveals what is hidden to those who love Him. He leads, guides, and protects His own. If you know you belong to Him, you can rejoice right now because your enemies will not triumph over you.

When they come against you, it will be their last hurrah. God is in your corner. It's a poor match-up. Your opponent is not even in your weight class. As the saints of old used to say, "Their arms are too short to box with God." Let them give you their best one-two punch. It doesn't matter. This fight is already fixed.

So it was with Elisha and the Syrians. God averted the fight before it even got underway. When Elisha prayed, God was able to sabotage the enemy's plan. "So when the Syrians came down to him, Elisha prayed to the LORD, and said, 'Strike this people, I pray, with blindness.' And He struck them with blindness according to the word of Elisha" (2 Kings 6:18 NKJV). Instantaneously, they were neutralized. Can you imagine how confused and afraid the Syrians must have been? At precisely the same moment, every one of them lost their ability to see. Ironically, they now needed the help of the one they had relentlessly pursued.

The prophet ushered them right out of Dothan and into Samaria, where they received their sight again (6:20). Under the circumstances, you might have thought Elisha and the Israelites would have retaliated. Instead, Elisha instructed the king of Israel to feed the Syrian soldiers and send them back from where they came, unharmed. Once they were released, they never came back. "So the bands of the Syrian raiders came no more into the land of Israel" (2 Kings 6:23 NKJV). Don't worry about a thing. Those who seek to stop you are already defeated.

❧ STAY ON THE WALL ❧

You may have wondered at one time or another, why God allows you to go through such difficult attacks. Can't He just pull you out and crush your enemies? He could, but that would not do you any good. He knows you have to learn how to navigate your way through life. There are some things you must experience to grow in your understanding. God may not immediately intervene every time something goes wrong.

Sometimes you have to dig deep and persevere through the persecution. Besides, how will you ever mature without enduring tough times? Take a moment to look back. You used to be gullible. Then you came face-to-face with persecution and you grew in wisdom. Think about that attack you thought would take you under, but you came out on top. It may not have been that long ago when you were in the throes of battle, uncertain about your future. Those who were against you were laughing at you and they thought it was over, but you came through it. A little bruised, but you came through. Somewhat shaken up, but you came through. A little fatigued, but you came through. A few restless nights, but you came through. The knowledge you now possess is a direct result of those hard struggles. Isn't God awesome? He alone is your shield, buckler, and your exceeding great reward. Psalm 18:2 says, "The LORD is my rock and my fortress and my deliverer; My God, my strength, in whom I will trust; My shield and the horn of my salvation, my stronghold" (NKJV).

I'm reminded of the triumphant story of Nehemiah. The book of Nehemiah, chapters 1–6, records how he discovers and fulfills his Divine assignment. It all began when he heard about the condition of the city of Jerusalem after King Nebuchadnezzar and the Babylonian army destroyed it (2 Chronicles 36:17-21). It grieved him so much to hear of the deplorable conditions of his homeland. He mourned, fasted, and prayed, until God gave him direction. Once he received confirmation from the Lord that this was indeed his assignment, he began putting the pieces in place to make it happen.

Initially, it seemed that everything was going smoothly. King Artaxerxes released Nehemiah from his duties as his personal cupbearer and gave him permission to rebuild Jerusalem's walls. He even wrote letters on Nehemiah's behalf, to ensure safety and provision for him. But things were about to change. Although God gave him favor with the King, he soon discovered that everyone wasn't in support of his mission. Once he galvanized the Jewish people and finally began working, the real trouble started.

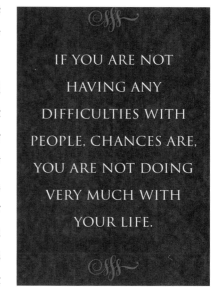

IF YOU ARE NOT HAVING ANY DIFFICULTIES WITH PEOPLE, CHANCES ARE, YOU ARE NOT DOING VERY MUCH WITH YOUR LIFE.

Anytime you stake your claim and start living out your purpose, that makes you a prime candidate for persecution. If you are not having any difficulties with people, chances are, you are not doing very much with your life. The moment you start walking in your calling, be aware that some folks may turn on you. Just as we covered at the beginning of the chapter, unless you have an interest in living the life of a puppet, you had better get used to some controversy.

Don't delude yourself into believing that you will always be praised and celebrated for your Kingdom-building efforts. Just because you are doing a good thing doesn't mean that everyone will perceive it that way. Somebody, somewhere, somehow, will find something wrong, sometime. Unless you plan to become a hermit and remain anonymous, you're going to have to learn to be strong. People don't talk about anonymous people, but they do ridicule world changers.

Even while detractors are railing against you, don't stop. You may be mistreated, misunderstood, and in some cases, even hated; don't let that concern you. Keep walking in God's ways and don't you dare give up. The Bible says, "If you faint in the day of adversity, Your strength is small" (Proverbs 24:10 NKJV).

Nehemiah and the Jews were derided and threatened. Nevertheless, they did not stop building. Instead, they gathered their weapons and continued laboring. "Those who built on the wall, and those who carried burdens, loaded themselves so that with one hand they worked at construction, and with the other held a weapon. Every one of the builders had his sword girded at his side as he built" (Nehemiah 4:17-18a NKJV).

Nehemiah and the Israelites were resolute. Are you? Understand that a mind to work is essential. It takes much effort to succeed at anything. Nobody is exempt. Approach your task soberly and you will fair well. On the other hand, if you think it's going to be all fun and games, you've got another thing coming. Aside from having to deal with outside opposition, you are going to have to condition your mind to roll up your sleeves and get to work.

Nehemiah knew that he had come to complete a job. Even though their lives were in danger, quitting was not an option. Whatever it took, they did it. In the most intense moments of persecution, they alternated positions, but they did not get off that wall. While some worked, others stood guard. Although many men were fearful of what their rivals would do, they stayed the course and refused to come down from building.

Please understand that Satan and his cohorts are working overtime to stop you from working to do anything toward the upward building of the Kingdom of God. Nothing would please him more than to get you to come down off the wall and change your decision to work for the Lord. I challenge you to plant your feet and set your face like stone to do God's will. Go in knowing you're going to face some resistance; persecution is inevitable when you commit your life to Christ. Paul lets us know that, "…all who desire to live godly in Christ Jesus will suffer persecution" (2 Timothy 3:12 NKJV). It's the cost of taking a stand for holiness and walking in your purpose.

I know it's not always easy to move forward in the face of resistance, but it is worth it. It can be very painful at times, but it is worth it. You may want to get off the wall, but stay. Ridiculers will no doubt come, but don't you dare cease and desist. Certainly, Nehemiah and the Israelites were ostracized by their critics. Still, they stayed the course.

But it so happened, when Sanballat heard that we were rebuilding the wall, that he was furious and very indignant, and mocked the Jews. And he spoke before his brethren and the army of Samaria, and said, "What are these feeble Jews doing? Will they fortify themselves? Will they offer sacrifices? Will they complete it in a day? Will they revive the stones from the heaps of rubbish—*stones* that are burned?"

Now Tobiah the Ammonite *was*beside him, and he said, "Whatever they build, if even a fox goes up *on it,* he will break down their stone wall."

Hear, O our God, for we are despised; turn their reproach on their own heads, and give them as plunder to a land of captivity! Do not cover their iniquity, and do not let their sin be blotted out from before You; for they have provoked *You* to anger before the builders.

So we built the wall, and the entire wall was joined together up to half its *height,* for the people had a mind to work. (Nehemiah 4:1-6 NKJV)

You don't have to worry, no matter how intense the attack. Let them speak against your vision. Let them try to discover ways to thwart your mission. You just keep declaring, "'No weapon formed against you shall prosper, And every tongue *which* rises against you in judgment You shall condemn. This *is* the heritage of the servants of the LORD, and their righteousness *is* from Me,' says the Lord" (Isaiah 54:17 NKJV).

All of the words your persecutors speak against you will come to nothing. And in the end, you will overcome, just as Nehemiah did. Remarkably, he led the Jews through the successful rebuilding of Jerusalem's walls in just fifty-two days (Nehemiah 6:15). They completed the rest of the project in only six months. It happened, all because he refused to let his enemies snatch away his purpose.

Do you see what you can accomplish, if you don't faint? You can stand with confidence knowing that you are on your way to a new place of destiny. Everyone may not like you when you get there, but so what. Some may try to upset the plan of God, but they will utterly fail. You may be confronted with vindictiveness and cruelty, but you will adjust. God has already ordained that you will triumph in the end. You do not have to be afraid of persecution. Just as God brought you out before, He will do it again. He will equip you to be victorious over every satanic attack. Not only will you win, you will experience blessing and increase in your life. Stay on the wall and stay in His will.

SEE THE OPPORTUNITY IN THE OPPOSITION

The devil is afraid of what is inside you. The powers of darkness do not want the seed of destiny you are carrying to flourish. That's why he works overtime to stop you from giving birth to the vision God has placed in you. He wants you to miscarry. He tries to intimidate you, silence you, and make you retreat. He knows that if he does not prohibit you from successfully completing your assignment, you will walk right into an awesome opportunity, to enlarge your borders for the Kingdom of God.

In the book of Esther, we find the story of a woman who did not allow the enemy to cancel her date with destiny. Just as she was growing accustomed to her new life as the Queen of Persia, she was faced with the responsibility of saving the lives of her people. Esther certainly did not anticipate that the Jews would be in danger of being killed. Suppose she was too intimidated to take on the challenge facing her? She had plenty of reasons to be afraid. No doubt, she felt overwhelmed and unsure of her ability to turn things around.

How could Esther possibly make a difference with so many obstacles confronting her? After all, she had quite a bit working against her:

- She had hidden her Jewish ethnicity from the king.
- Haman, the very man, who initiated the attack against the Jews, just so happened to be her husband's right hand man.
- In order to get time alone to speak to the king, protocol said she had to be summoned. If she simply barged in unsolicited, she could be put to death.
- An irreversible decree had gone out from the king for the annihilation of the Jewish people.

It seemed to be a foregone conclusion that she and all her people would die. Why should she even take on a hopeless assignment such as this one? The opposition seemed much too great. Besides, who did she think she was? She didn't have the right or the clout to take her complaint before the king. She did not want to go the way of Vashti, the last queen, that's for sure. What should she do? The insightful words of her cousin, Mordecai, would help her choose.

"Do not think in your heart that you will escape in the king's palace any more than all the other Jews. For if you remain completely silent at this time, relief and deliverance will arise for the Jews from another place, but you and your father's house will perish. Yet who knows whether you have come to the kingdom for such a time as this?" (Esther 4:14 NKJV).

He wanted Esther to focus on her purpose instead of the peril and persecution that was confronting her. What did she have to lose? If she approached the king, he might potentially show mercy. If she did nothing at all, however, she and all her people faced certain death. Sometimes, it's not until your back is up against the wall that you are able to see the blessing amid the turmoil. If you persevere through persecution, God will reveal His plan.

Esther had no way of knowing that out of this situation would come an amazing opportunity. She would be able to bring deliverance and assistance to thousands of people on the verge of losing their lives. Although Esther could've been killed in the process, God had uniquely equipped her for the task.

God never said your journey would be trouble-free. Why not go ahead and trust God and move forward? You will be amazed by what He will do on your behalf. You don't have time to sit around second-guessing yourself. It is your season to do what He has called you to do. Satan wants to control your mind and show you all of the roadblocks in the way of destiny. He will tell you *why you can't, why you shouldn't, why it's not wise, why it's a mistake, why it's wishful thinking.* If you listen to his

GOD NEVER SAID YOUR JOURNEY WOULD BE TROUBLE-FREE.

lies, he will steal the heritage that rightfully belongs to you. Open your eyes and see the hand of God at work.

Be bold and courageous, knowing that you already have the victory. Don't back down; move forward. Can you imagine the genocide that would have taken place if Esther had been too afraid to forge ahead? Thankfully, she made the choice to believe God and in the process, discovered her life's purpose. God had already given Esther the ability and the connections to do what He specifically chose her for. All she needed was the courage.

Are you bold enough to take on your assignment? Don't let Satan get in your ear and talk you out of a major blessing. He is sneaky, subtle, and sly, so don't be deceived by him. He wants your mind. Check your thoughts and make sure they line up with the word of God. "For the weapons of our warfare *are* not carnal but mighty in God for pulling down strongholds, casting down arguments and every high thing that exalts itself against the knowledge of God, bringing every thought into captivity to the obedience of Christ" (2 Corinthians 10:4-5 NKJV).

Bring those contrary thoughts under subjection. Surely, Esther had to control hers. Had she let the enemy rule her thinking, he could have stopped her progress. Then she would have never seen the hand of God at work in her life. You too, must be careful not to succumb to the cunning and crafty ways of the enemy. The devil doesn't grab you by the throat, pin you to the wall, and make you believe his lies. Instead, he eases his way in. Little by little, he plays on your psyche and plants things in your mind. That is how he gets you to agree with his way of thinking.

This is exactly what he did to Eve in the Garden of Eden. Genesis 3:1 records, "Now the serpent was more cunning than any beast of the field which the LORD God had made. And he said to the woman, 'Has God indeed said, 'You shall not eat of every tree of the garden?'" (NKJV). Now, stop right there. What did the serpent do? Just that quickly, he planted a seed of doubt in Eve's mind. He was working to gradually win her over to his way of thinking. He took her step by step. That is his method. Don't ever forget it. If you are not careful, he will play with your mind. Before you know it, he will have you believing that his thoughts are your own. You'll be engaged in a full on conversation with the enemy, posing as your ally.

When Satan saw his opportunity, he seized it. "Then the serpent said to the woman, "You will not surely die. For God knows that in the day you eat of it your eyes will be opened, and you will be like God, knowing good and evil" (3:4-5 NKJV). Eve bought into the lie, convinced her husband, and the rest is history. Satan won that time, but don't let him get the victory over you. Don't give him the satisfaction. When he tries to wage war against your mind, rebuke him. Otherwise, you run the risk of allowing him to steal your destiny.

He wants to make you doubt God's Word. He attempts to weaken your resolve. He wants to convince you that it's time to give up on your purpose. He does this so you don't see the opportunities that lie before you; so you won't recognize your God-given ability to possess the land of promise; so you do not believe that you have the favor to lay hold of everything God has for you.

Esther did not know she had the ability to do what she did, until she did it. She broke out of her shell, took a risk, and turned the situation in her favor. The king sent out a new decree that allowed the Jews to defend themselves in battle, but it never would have happened if Esther had not chosen to press on in the midst of persecution.

If you are going through an attack right now that you don't quite understand, you really need to praise God in the middle of it. There is more to it than the momentary struggle. Rejoice, because the enemy is just setting you up for a blessing. As God's favored child, He is working for you behind the scenes. The door is open. Now walk through it. This whole situation may be paving your path to purpose and prosperity. It all begins when you see the opportunity in the opposition and persevere through the persecution.

CHAPTER 6

STAY CONNECTED

I don't want good connections.
I want God connections.

UNKNOWN

As you move into your place of promise, I want you to be mindful of all the things you have read in this book about people and relationships. In Chapter 3, you learned how to identify and rid yourself of dead weight and dream killers. In Chapter 5, you discovered how vital it is to recognize the people Satan has assigned to impede your progress. In this chapter, I want to help you understand the importance of staying connected to God, so He can connect you to the right people. This is central to the discovery of your life's purpose because God works through people to accomplish His plans. The 17th Century poet, John Donne said, "No man is an island unto himself." Not one of us on this earth can survive without the assistance of another. We are interdependent. We all need help.

It's a fact of life that there are others who *know more than you know, have more than you have,* and *already are where you want to be.* These are the people who are capable of teaching you things you must know, in order to carry out God's will. Does that mean you should indiscriminately associate with anyone who seemingly has more knowledge and more "stuff" than you? To that I emphatically say, "Absolutely not!" That is just not wise. There are many individuals who are materially rich, but morally bankrupt. Please don't miss the point by misunderstanding what I'm saying.

Every connection is not a Divine connection and in this season of your life you do not want to make the mistake of linking up with just anybody, as a means to an end. 1 Corinthians 15:33 teaches us that bad company [connections] corrupt good manners. Essentially, if you walk with the wise, you'll become wise; walk with the stupid and you'll become…well, you know the rest. (See Proverbs 13:20.) In our high-tech society, it's easy to connect to anyone virtually, anywhere in the world, in a few seconds. But, just because you know how to reach out and touch someone, does not mean you should be so quick to do so.

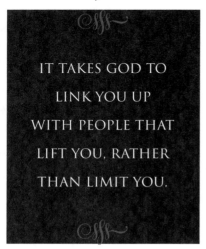

IT TAKES GOD TO LINK YOU UP WITH PEOPLE THAT LIFT YOU, RATHER THAN LIMIT YOU.

It takes God to link you up with people that lift you, rather than limit you. Consider it from this perspective. New relationships are like marriages in that they *should not be entered into lightly and inadvisably.* Don't rush to get hitched, without full assurance from the Lord that it is the right thing to do. Only He knows all the factors affecting whether an alliance will be successful, so listen to His voice. It is not your job to play matchmaker. If you are not careful, you will base your criteria on all the wrong things and end up hurt. Many people place too much emphasis on insignificant details, while neglecting more substantive matters.

They ask questions like: Who do they know? What kind of car do they drive? Where do they live? How much money do they make a year? How do they look? Let me advise you on something that can save you some serious trouble. Outward appearances will deceive you; don't get caught up in what you think you know. You need to be sure and very sure about what you are getting into before you take the plunge. You know the old saying, "you can't judge a book by its cover." The Bible says it this way, "For *the LORD does* not *see* as man sees; for man looks at the outward appearance, but the LORD looks at the heart" (1 Samuel 16:7b). In the previous chapter, we discovered that only God knows what is going on in those hidden places. That's why you need to trust His counsel. He will never steer you in the wrong direction. That's a promise.

Don't make the mistake the children of Israel made back in the book of 1 Samuel, chapter 8. They wanted a king to rule over them so they could be like all the other nations. They were frustrated with Samuel's sons, Joel and Abijah, the two corrupt judges who were in power at that time. Essentially, Israel had grown tired of the ungodly ways of their leaders who had "turned aside after dishonest gain, took bribes, and perverted justice" (8:3 NKJV).

The children of Israel decided to take matters into their own hands, thoroughly convinced that they knew exactly what needed to be done. Rather than consulting God about the problem, the elders of Israel got together and came up with what they believed was a feasible plan. Do not ever make permanent decisions based on temporary circumstances. If you allow yourself to be governed by your feelings, you will make rash decisions. Your emotions are unreliable and ever-changing. What makes sense in the heat of the moment may prove to be irrational later.

Always seek the Lord before you make a move. "Pray without ceasing" (1 Thessalonians 5:17 NKJV). If you don't, your feelings will lead you down a path you may later bemoan. You must fix your eyes upon the only One who never changes and His name is Jesus. Unfortunately, the elders of Israel forged ahead with their plan to confront the prophet Samuel. They told him, "Look, you are old, and your sons do not walk in your ways. Now make us a king to judge us like all the nations" (1 Samuel 8:5 NKJV). It seemed like the right thing to do, but only God knew what the real outcome would be.

So, the Lord spoke to Samuel and said, "...you shall solemnly forewarn them, and show them the behavior of the king who will reign over them" (1Samuel 8:9b NKJV). Take a look at the litany of ways future kings would cause undue stress and hardship for the Israelites.

> Samuel told the people who were asking for a king what the LORD had said: If you have a king, this is how he will treat you. He will force your sons to join his army. Some of them will ride in his chariots, some will serve in the cavalry, and others will run ahead of his own chariot. Some of them will be officers in charge of a

thousand soldiers, and others will be in charge of fifty. Still others will have to farm the king's land and harvest his crops, or make weapons and parts for his chariots. Your daughters will have to make perfume or do his cooking and baking. The king will take your best fields, as well as your vineyards, and olive orchards and give them to his own officials. He will also take a tenth of your grain and grapes and give it to his officers and officials.

The king will take your slaves and your best young men and your donkeys and make them do his work. He will also take a tenth of your sheep and goats. You will become the king's slaves, and you will finally cry out for the LORD to save you from the king you wanted. But the LORD won't answer your prayers. (1 Samuel 8:10-18 CEV)

God wanted them to see the reality of the situation would be quite the opposite of what they were hoping for. They really had no idea what they were getting themselves into. "There is a way *that seems* right to a man, But its end is the way of death" (Proverbs 14:12 NKJV). Have you ever been there? You may have been so sure you knew what you were doing, until you did it. Then you were sorry. It didn't turn out at all the way you

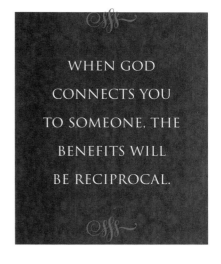

WHEN GOD CONNECTS YOU TO SOMEONE, THE BENEFITS WILL BE RECIPROCAL.

expected it to. You hooked up with a bad connection and then ended up being taken advantage of. When God connects you to someone, the benefits will be reciprocal. You will not have to worry about a lopsided relationship, where you are constantly giving and never receiving.

God was telling Israel that this whole arrangement would be very one-sided. They would always be on the losing end of the deal. Even still, they were unrelenting in their demands. They flat out rejected God's warnings. "Nevertheless the people refused to obey the voice of Samuel; and they said, 'No, but we will have a king over us...that our king may judge us and go out before us and fight our battles'" (1 Samuel 8:19-20 NKJV).

Sadly, they didn't realize they were not rejecting Samuel and his sons. They were going directly against God, Who had fought for them and protected them so many times before. Though God knew they were headed down the wrong path, He did not force them to heed His voice. Neither will He constrain you and me. We must willingly obey and follow God with full confidence that He will take care of us. If you will only be still and have faith in God's sovereignty, He will connect you to those *He* has hand-picked to take you to the next level. Don't you want to go?

By His power, God is about to transition you into an entirely new and better environment. You do not have to force things to happen. You do not need to hobnob, name drop, or network, as the world does. God is sending the right people into your life without any assistance from you. Just stay connected to Him. Until now, perhaps you've been attached to the wrong people. You may have thought you had to make things happen. You may have got a little too anxious. You may have forgotten the Word of the Lord that says, "Be anxious for nothing, but in everything by prayer and supplication, with thanksgiving, let your requests be made known to God" (Philippians 4:6 NKJV).

Gone are the days of indiscriminate relationships. It's a whole new season now. You need to be ready for some serious changes in your life. It is time to send those bad connections a final disconnect notice and tell them it's over. Tell them you are hanging up. They have kept your line tied up for too long. The one call you want to answer has been on hold because of them. You can't keep the One who called you waiting any longer. If by chance there are still some people in your life, that need to be released, here's what you do.

Dial their numbers one last time and say goodbye. Then burn that little black book. What do you have to lose anyway? All this time they have been costing you everything, but giving you nothing in return. They have been calling during peak hours and wasting your daytime minutes. Here's your chance to get singular in your thinking. What I mean by that is you need to make up your mind about what you are going to do. Who are you going to choose? Do you want familiar connections or Divine connections? Make a decision. God, the Operator, wants to change your number. If you let Him do it, the next time your old acquaintances call, they'll hear this message: "I'm sorry. The number you have reached has recently been changed. No further information is available." You've reached a juncture when God is forming some new alliances on your behalf. Strap in and enjoy the ride.

❧ REPORT TO BAGGAGE CLAIM ❧

Ask yourself, "Am I healthy enough to maximize Divine connections? Am I spiritually, mentally, and emotionally whole? Am I still holding on to unresolved issues from my past?" Before you can successfully embrace new people, you must first deal with your old baggage. If you don't, you will end up ruining relationships, burning bridges, and eventually, self-destructing. Granted, there is a certain level of anxiety associated with accepting new people and things. It's quite normal to be uneasy while trying to find your place. It is no fun being the "new kid on the block." You feel somewhat displaced and isolated. You don't know who to talk to. You are not familiar with the code of conduct in that particular environment. It is difficult to be the outsider.

At some point, however, you have to branch out and open yourself up; that is, if you ever expect to broaden your circle of influence. I know that change can be intimidating, but the alternative is much worse. When you shut everybody out, you also box yourself in. When you choose to be reclusive, you unwittingly distance yourself from the very people who are assigned to help you fulfill your purpose. It is quite easy to close yourself off from people, once you have been wounded. It's your defensive strategy. It seems like the safest thing to do. You may reason that if you don't let anyone get close to you again, you won't have to worry about being hurt anymore. But do not disengage and disconnect. That is not the answer.

A much better approach is to focus on all the positive things God is doing. Stop rehashing those times when you endured injustice and unfair treatment. Choose to be optimistic, even after your heart has been broken and your trust breached. Whether you sustained the injury days, weeks, months, or years ago, make a deliberate decision not to let it get the best of you.

I have a poignant memory of an unpleasant incident that happened to me when I was just a young boy in the fourth grade. It all occurred one day after school, when one of my schoolmates decided to attack me for no apparent reason. I remember him venomously yelling and calling me, "Half breed!" I did not even know what the derogatory term meant at the time. But judging from his angry tone of voice and facial expression, I perceived that *half breed* likely was not a good thing.

As you can imagine, I was completely caught off guard by the whole occurrence. Before I got a chance to really process what was going on… Wham! He hit me upside the head with a stick and I mean he hit me hard. So forcefully, in fact, I nearly passed out. Oh, but when I collected myself…I grabbed him by his shirt and lifted him off the ground. While he dangled in mid-air trembling like a leaf in the wind, I stared him squarely in the eyes. Then, I told him through clenched teeth, "If you ever put your hands on me again, as long as you live, you will be very, very sorry." I slowly lowered him to the ground. As soon as his feet hit the pavement, he ran home as fast as he could. When I looked around, all my friends were chanting my name. "Lawrence! Lawrence! Lawrence!" Then I watched as each of my enemies, one-by-one, backed away nervously, cowering in fear. Man, did I feel powerful that day!

Okay, okay…at least that's the way I like to remember it. After partially regaining consciousness, here is what *really* happened. I felt my legs turn to rubber. My knees buckled beneath me. I was dazed and woozy. I stumbled aimlessly, while watching tiny stars dance all around my head. As if that wasn't enough, a gigantic knot formed in the place where I had been clubbed. Thankfully, the school monitor came and dragged the kid off to the principal's office. *Finally,* I thought, *justice will be served!*

Well…not so much. As it turns out, the boy's father was a prominent doctor in the city. All he got was a tap on the hand, while I went home with a lump on the head and a pain in the heart. I felt dejected, angry, and confused. I wondered, *Why did that happen to me? Is something wrong with me?* It didn't make much sense, but at the same time, it had a deeply negative impact on my psyche. I was not just physically bruised. I was emotionally wounded.

I remember not wanting to go back to school. I struggled with feelings of displacement. I felt a bit insecure. Even though I had friends who genuinely cared for me, it was still very difficult to overcome the emotional injury. Over time, I would come to know the delivering power of the Holy Spirit, but when it first happened, I tried managing the myriad of emotions on my own. It wasn't easy.

Though I wanted to at times, I didn't crawl into a shell and totally shun the outside world. Neither can you. If you do that, Satan will use your anxiety and fear to gain a stronghold on your mind. He will cause you to pull the plug on valuable and viable relationships. You will abort your destiny and hinder your productivity. You will isolate those who really do have your best interest at heart. You will be shifty and shady, inconsistent and intolerant, unpredictable and uncontrollable. That's not what God wants for you.

He does not want to see you ruin opportunities to excel because you have not released the emotional resentment associated with situations from your past. Whatever you're dealing with needs to be put in check. You have to get your mind right so you can enjoy the outpouring of God's goodness. It is time to turn the page on painful memories and begin a new chapter in your life. Perhaps you were mocked and scorned. Consequently, you developed a complex. Believe me; I know firsthand what it's like.

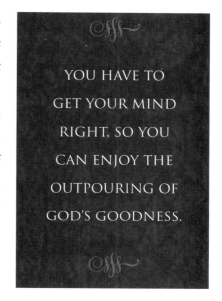

YOU HAVE TO GET YOUR MIND RIGHT, SO YOU CAN ENJOY THE OUTPOURING OF GOD'S GOODNESS.

I was picked on as a child for being "too thin." My peers would call me *skinny, stick,* and *pencil.* Then to make matters worse, the taunting continued into my teenager years. Whenever I walked by, some of my friends would look me in the face and without saying a word, simply hold up their pointer fingers to signify just how skinny I was. They thought it was a hilarious gesture. Though I pretended not to care, it tore me up each time they did it.

What I just shared may or may not seem all that significant to you, but the constant taunting took its toll on me. It got so bad that I was too ashamed to wear shorts, because I didn't want anyone to see my scrawny legs. As a result of the teasing, gaining weight became my personal obsession. I tried everything: weight gain powder, protein supplements, sugar, squats, bench pressing, and anything else I could think of. No matter how hard I tried, nothing worked.

Thankfully, I'm able to laugh about it now—I'm not skinny any longer, but it wasn't at all funny then.

❧ BUILD GODLY RELATIONSHIPS ❧

What about you? Perchance, there is something you are not quite able to laugh about yet. It still eats away at you. You continually struggle with it. It keeps you from being receptive to new people and things. Be real about it. You are not alone. Many individuals walk around with a poor self-image, because others disparaged them, but you can be delivered. You can live, love, and thrive again. If you open up, you can discover how kind and generous people can truly be. Identify your baggage, so you don't punish others for what someone else did to you. You do not want to make the mistake of unceremoniously dismissing Divine connections, just because you are too afraid to put your heart on the line again. Don't fall into the trap of the enemy. He wants you to disconnect, but don't do it.

Choose instead to get out there and start over again. Pursue your purpose. Adopt a new attitude and a better perspective. Your life philosophy cannot be, "If I don't expect anything, then I can't be disappointed." Let hope and faith in God fill your heart. You can't burn bridges with people and then turn on your heels and walk out in a blaze of glory. You will end up alone and unfulfilled. Conversely, build bridges, relationships, and alliances. Stay connected. You might have to talk yourself through it, but stay on course. Don't you dare allow yourself to destroy what God is doing. He is ordering your steps and orchestrating your life. Give Him free reign to assist you and stop worrying.

As you continue moving forward in the strength of the Lord, know and be confident that He is with you. "Have I not commanded you? Be strong and of good courage; do not be afraid, nor be dismayed, for the LORD your God is with you wherever you go" (Joshua 1:9 NKJV).

When you feel like running away, just keep putting one foot in front of the other. Grin and bear it. Grit your teeth. You have come too far now to turn around. Pray...but no bolting allowed. Breathe. Count to ten. Do shoulder rolls. Crack your knuckles. Wring your hands together. Wipe the sweat from your palms. Cry. Feel the fear and ignore it. Now...slowly . . . remove the bolt locks off the door and let someone in. It will get easier after awhile, but you have to start somewhere. Don't waste anymore time profiling people, seeing if they look anything like the composite sketch you have in your mind. Trust the Lord to lead you by his peace with your relationships.

Surely, you can't possibly think you know someone's "M. O.," simply because they remind you of a person from your past who was crazy. That does not mean *they* are crazy. You cannot write off all men because you had one bad relationship, or mistrust all women because one turned out to be disloyal. Tell yourself as often as you need to that, "Everybody is not insane. Everybody is not out to get me. Everybody is not plotting my demise."

It reminds me of a lesson that was constantly reinforced by my parents during my developmental years. You see, when I got into trouble at school, my teachers would sometimes call home to report my inappropriate behavior. Certainly I could not sit back and become the helpless victim of cruel injustice and slander. Never! I would rise up and sway the opinions of my parents. I would courageously defend my honor. I would eloquently articulate the reasons why this ruthless sabotage must be stopped. Now envision me, with all the conviction and genuine emotion I could muster, spewing out, "It's not true. You don't understand. They…they just don't like me. Please listen. I'm telling you, they're prejudiced."

You've probably heard that before. And apparently, my parents had too. Needless to say, they were unimpressed by my overly dramatized speeches. Their response would always be the same, "Lawrence, everybody's not out to get you."

Perhaps, you may be wondering, "How do I know if someone is trustworthy? How can I be sure this is a Divine connection?" God will reveal it to you. You'll know in your spirit. You don't have to rely on a hunch, a gut feeling, women's intuition, or an itchy palm. These are not foolproof methods of gaining insight into someone's character. If you come from a superstitious family, you need to disregard all of the nonsense you have learned along the way. Only the Holy Spirit gives genuine revelation of truth. Remember, discernment and suspicion are two very different things. I want you to highlight the previous sentence and never forget it.

You have to stop being carnal in your approach to life and begin asking God for Divine wisdom. "If any of you lacks wisdom, let him ask of God, who gives to all liberally and without reproach, and it will be given to him" (James 1:5 NKJV). It is so important to recognize that none of us, without Godly insight, has the ability to rightly judge matters. All of us, on some level, are predisposed to biases and opinions which distort our perceptions of people and situations. We all operate from unique paradigms that reflect the sum total of all we have learned and experienced. Only God is able to filter out the contamination of our social conditioning and help us see clearly.

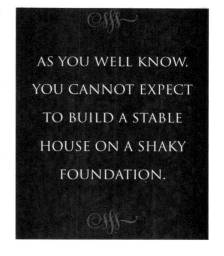

As you well know, you cannot expect to build a stable house on a shaky foundation. Likewise, you cannot draw solid conclusions about persons, places, and situations, based on faulty premises. You will end up severely misguided and off course. You will think you are being judicious and prudent, when you're really being paranoid and ridiculous. "Through wisdom a house is built, And by understanding it is established; By knowledge the rooms are filled With all precious and pleasant riches" (Proverbs 24:3-4 NKJV). As you seek the Lord for knowledge and understanding, He will bless you abundantly.

This is precisely what we see exemplified in the life of Solomon, who was given the lofty task of succeeding the throne of his father David (1 Kings 1:28-53). He was young, inexperienced, and in great need of God's direction in order to fulfill the numerous tasks that were before him (1 Kings 3:7-9). God knew that Solomon was greatly in need of His help, so the Lord spoke to him and said, "Ask! What shall I give you?" (1 Kings 3:5b NKJV). Solomon responded to God by saying, "...give to Your servant an understanding heart to judge Your people, that I may discern between good and evil. For who is able to judge this great people of Yours?" (1 Kings 3:9 NKJV).

The Bible records in verses 11 and 12 that his answer pleased God so much, He gave Solomon more wisdom than any man that preceded him and any that would come after him. "...see, I have given you a wise and understanding heart, so that there has not been anyone like you before you, nor shall any like you arise after you" (1 Kings 3:12b NKJV). Let me point out that during this conversation with God, Solomon was merely dreaming. "At Gibeon the LORD appeared to Solomon in a dream by night; and God said, 'Ask! What shall I give you?'" (1 Kings 3:5 NKJV). Even while asleep, God was giving Solomon insight into His will and plan for his life. He promised in the dream to bestow great wisdom, riches, and honor upon him. And all that God shared with Solomon in his sleep came to fruition.

Just as God was with Solomon, He will also be with you. I know you may feel overwhelmed when occupying new roles and venturing into other territories, but God will uphold you. "Fear not, for I *am* with you; be not dismayed, for I *am* your God. I will strengthen you, Yes, I will help you, I will uphold you with My righteous right hand" (Isaiah 41:10 NKJV). Just place your confidence in the Omniscient One. He will not let you fall. He will show you everything you need to know.

That is precisely what He did for Solomon when he had to resolve a heated dispute between two harlots in 1 Kings 3:16-27. This particular case was quite interesting. Both women had given birth to brand new baby boys, just three days apart. The problem arose when one woman rolled over on her son and suffocated him. In the middle of the night, she snuck over to the unsuspecting mother's bed, stole her healthy baby boy, and put her dead son in his place. It was treacherous.

Solomon had to distinguish between the real mother and the baby snatcher. Who was telling the truth? Who was lying? How could he make the right decision? He had no tangible evidence. There were no eyewitnesses to the crime. Obviously, he could not rely solely on the report of either woman, since both were claiming ownership of the baby with equal passion and intensity. This situation was seemingly irreconcilable and unsolvable. If Solomon were trusting in his own wisdom, he likely would have been stuck in a quandary.

What made the difference was that he was armed with the wisdom of God. As a result, Solomon was about to crack this case wide open. Interestingly, he proposed cutting the baby in half and dividing his remains equally between the two mothers. One woman eagerly consented, while the other cried out in protest. The latter could not bear the thought of any harm being inflicted upon the innocent child. At that moment, everything became clear to Solomon. He ruled in favor of the one willing to give up the child, rather than see him die. "And all Israel heard of the judgment which the king had rendered; and they feared the king, for they saw that the wisdom of God *was* in him to administer justice" (1 Kings 3:28 NKJV).

He was able to judge rightly because God illuminated his understanding. You can be confident that when the Lord leads you, He will show you things that are hidden to others. You won't have to make assumptions. The answers will become obvious. You don't have to worry about being deceived by individuals who lack integrity. God will expose them. When He is on your side, the traps and snares set by the enemy will not work against you.

On the other hand, don't slip into the habit of always thinking the worst of people. I told you earlier, everyone is not against you. You cannot go around looking at people sideways and sizing them up based on your preconceived notions. If you are not careful, you will be saying ridiculous things like: "I just got a negative vibe when she walked by me. Anybody who wears that kind of suit can't be trusted." "His eyes shifted a little to the left while he was talking to me. That means he was lying." "I'm telling you her right eye kept twitching the whole time, so I think she was covering something up." "Anybody who smiles that much, can't be no good."

Stop making nonsensical judgments about people. Gather yourself and learn to make the distinction between good sense and nonsense. Don't mistake one for the other. I'm not proposing that you ignore every sign. If someone chokes you in the middle of a conversation, *that's* a red flag. If someone walks up behind you with a ski mask on, and says, "Give me all your money," *that's* a red flag. But if you choose not to associate with someone because they have on the same blue sweater as the last person who did you wrong, then you need to immediately report to baggage claim. You get my drift.

Before you draw any conclusions about anything or anyone, ask yourself, "Have I consulted God? Did He speak to me about this person? Do I really know anything about them or is my emotional baggage getting in the way?" This will help you not to wrongly judge people and things, based on outward appearances. I admonish you to seek God for balance, direction, and peace. Remain steadfast in prayer; be open to new ideas and diverse people. "My son, pay attention to my wisdom; Lend your ear to my understanding, That you may preserve discretion, And your lips may keep knowledge" (Proverbs 5:1-2 NKJV).

"Wisdom is the principal thing; Therefore get wisdom. And in all your getting, get understanding. Exalt her, and she will promote you; She will bring you honor, when you embrace her. She will place on your head an ornament of grace; A crown of glory she will deliver to you" (Proverbs 4:7-9 NKJV).

LET GOD DO THE CONNECTING

God has mapped out your journey, and you just have to follow the path. Things have already been set in order— trust Him. All the pieces of the puzzle will come together for you at precisely the right moment. Nothing has been left

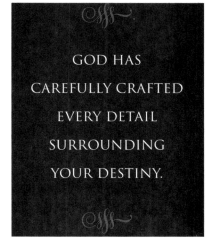

GOD HAS CAREFULLY CRAFTED EVERY DETAIL SURROUNDING YOUR DESTINY.

to chance. The date, time, person, and place has already been assigned. God has carefully crafted every detail surrounding your destiny. He did not leave anything out. He knows your personality and style, your likes and dislikes, your strengths and weaknesses, your hopes and dreams. He understands you through and through, with all of your nuances and idiosyncrasies. God is the only One who can effectively link you to the appropriate people. He has designated specific individuals to assist you in the fulfillment of His plan for your life. Let God do the connecting.

Don't try it on your own. It just won't work, and you will make a mess. Only He knows the route you must take. And without a doubt, it will be different from the path you would have chosen for yourself. "'For My thoughts *are* not your thoughts, Nor *are* your ways My ways,' says the LORD.' For as the heavens are higher than the earth, So are My ways higher than your ways, And My thoughts than your thoughts'" (Isaiah 55:8-9 NKJV). You may as well rest in Him and stop trying to figure Him out. "Oh, the depth of the riches both of the wisdom and knowledge of God! How unsearchable *are* His judgments and His ways past finding out! *For who has known the mind of the LORD? Or who has become His counselor?*" (Romans 11:33-34 NKJV).

Though He may not reveal everything on His mind *to* you, He is always mindful *of* you. He wants only the best for your life. Don't go through life searching, struggling, and striving unnecessarily. Simply rest upon His promise. Don't frustrate yourself trying to do His job for Him, and don't waste your energy, spinning your wheels and making no progress. Relax, it does not matter how it looks right now. He will most assuredly send key connections your way.

If God did it for the Apostle Paul, He will do it for you. Paul certainly did not begin as a defender of the faith. On the contrary, he was known as Saul of Tarsus and was a notorious persecutor of the early Christian church. We first encounter him in the book of the Acts of the Apostles as he stood by, watching unsympathetically, while Stephen, the first Christian martyr, was stoned to death for the sake of the Gospel (Acts 7:58).

Essentially, Saul hated Jewish Christians, and they were absolutely terrified of him. The relationship was so contentious because Saul was a very influential Pharisee on a relentless mission to preserve the integrity of traditional Jewish customs. He believed that the Christians were in direct opposition to the Law of God according to the Old Testament, and he felt that it was his duty to protect the sanctity of religious traditions. He was well known throughout Jerusalem for arresting Christians and hauling them off to the authorities to be punished for their rebellion. The irony of all of this is that, in his mind, he committed such cruel acts against Christians as an expression of his zeal for God (Philippians 3:6). He thought he was doing a righteous and noble thing. I'm sure you've heard it said that, "you can be sincere, yet sincerely wrong." That would be the perfect way to characterize Saul; that is, before he came to know Jesus Christ.

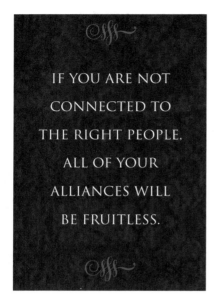

IF YOU ARE NOT CONNECTED TO THE RIGHT PEOPLE, ALL OF YOUR ALLIANCES WILL BE FRUITLESS.

His extensive training and key relationships put him in the "Who's Who" of Israel. Saul was educated under the great Jewish scholar, Gamaliel, the most outstanding rabbinical teacher of that time (Acts 5:34; 22:3). He was circumcised exactly as Jewish Law prescribed, and he was a very eloquent speaker. By worldly standards, he had everything going for him…everything except his true purpose. It really does not matter how much money, respect, and notoriety you have. If you are not living your Divine purpose, it means nothing. If you are not connected to the right people, all of your alliances will be fruitless. If your pockets are full, but your spirit is empty, what good is it? "For what will it profit a man if he gains the whole world, and loses his own soul?" (Mark 8:36 NKJV). Only the Lord can make your life significant. Nothing has any value or worth without Him. If you don't want your existence to be in vain, then let Him reign supreme. Give Him complete control.

That is what God wanted from Saul. His plan was firmly in place to engraft him into the Christian brotherhood. Isn't it interesting to note that the very people Saul was persecuting were the gatekeepers to his destiny? Saul, the *persecutor,* was about to become Paul the *proselyte.* God was going to use his gifts to expand the Christian church, and amazingly, he would write two thirds of the New Testament.

One day, while Saul was riding his donkey on the road to Damascus, he was introduced to Jesus Christ Himself. "When Saul had almost reached Damascus, a bright light from heaven suddenly flashed around him. He fell to the ground and heard a voice that said, 'Saul! Saul! Why are you so cruel to me?' 'Who are you?' Saul asked.

'I am Jesus,' the Lord answered. 'I am the one you are so cruel to. Now get up and go into the city, where you will be told what to do.'

The men with Saul stood there speechless. They had heard the voice, but they had not seen anyone. Saul got up from the ground, and when he opened his eyes, he could not see a thing" (Acts 9:3-8 CEV).

After this experience, Saul was never again the same; he was instantaneously a new man. Though he lost his natural sight, he gained his spiritual sight. He had to first go blind before he could really see. What the Lord had done for him was remarkable, but now what?

He was in serious need of Divine direction and favor. He had a slight problem, you see. Although his nature was instantly changed, his reputation remained the same. How was he ever going to gain credibility with the Christians? What could he possibly say to change their minds? Would anybody even believe his conversion? Would they forgive him for all of the turmoil and pain he had caused them? I have a better question for you, is there anything too hard for the Lord? (Genesis 18:14 NKJV).

Aren't you glad that God is not limited by your past? It does not matter who you used to be, what you used to do, where you used to go, and how you used to act. By His power, He is giving you access to the Divine connections you need to bring glory to His name. He is not worried about what others think of you. He is not focused on whether they like you. Remember, whether people approve of you is not important, as long as you stay connected to God, His purpose will prevail. You may not have the credentials for the circle you are called to infiltrate, but it doesn't matter. God is going to arrest the attention of those who can open doors that would otherwise be closed in your face. Just step aside, let God do the connecting, and watch what happens.

The Apostle Paul's life is a true testimony of what God can do. The Lord singled out a man named Ananias to assist Paul, who was originally called "Saul," during the first phase of his transition. "Now there was a certain disciple at Damascus named Ananias; and to him the Lord said in a vision, 'Ananias.' And he said, 'Here I am, Lord.' So the Lord *said* to him, 'Arise and go to the street called Straight, and inquire at the house of Judas for *one* called Saul of Tarsus, for behold, he is praying'" (Acts 9:10-11 NKJV). Now, when

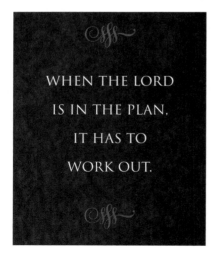

WHEN THE LORD IS IN THE PLAN, IT HAS TO WORK OUT.

Ananias heard what God wanted him to do, he was not enthusiastic about it. He said, "Lord, I have heard from many about this man, how much harm he has done to Your saints in Jerusalem. And here he has authority from the chief priests to bind all who call on Your name" (Acts 9:13–14 NKJV). Saul was a very high profile figure. In this case, however, it did not seem to be working in his favor.

Even though Ananias had heard about the terrible things Saul had done, the Lord already knew he would obey. Pay close attention to what happened here. The Lord, in His infinite wisdom, knew that Ananias would follow His directives, albeit reluctantly at first. That's why He chose him. Do you see the importance of allowing God to do the connecting? He covers all the bases. You don't have to worry about a thing. When the Lord is in the plan, it has to work out. Take your hands off of the situation. It's way over your head and out of your league. You don't even know where to begin. If you try to get things done through your own ability, you will fail miserably. But when you let God do it, He fights your battles for you. He makes things easy. He makes people bless you that don't even like you. He will prepare a table before you right in the presence of your enemies (Psalm 23:5).

Isn't He good? I'm telling you, when God is ready to bring you into your place of destiny, you don't have to worry about how everything will come together. Just know that He is on your side. You may not see it, but when you least expect it, He will send people to come looking for you, just the way He sent Ananias to Saul. Blessings will chase you down and overtake you (Deuteronomy 28:2). It is only a matter of time. The question is not if, but when? Stay out of doubt and just wait on Him.

Saul had to wait and he was without sight, food, or drink for three days (Acts 9:9). Then Ananias showed up and said, "Brother Saul, the Lord Jesus, who appeared to you on the road as you came, has sent me that you may receive your sight and be filled with the

Holy Spirit" (Acts 9:17b NKJV). That day Saul received the Holy Spirit and his sight was restored. He immediately began proclaiming the Good News in the synagogues and declaring that Jesus Christ was indeed the Son of God. This transition did not take place without controversy and persecution. It was by no means easy. The Jews were not happy about Saul's conversion and they plotted to kill him (9:23).

When Paul was rejected in Damascus, he went to Jerusalem and tried to join the disciples. Initially, it did not go very well. The Christians did not want to hear from Paul either. As far as they were concerned, he had an ulterior motive and was up to no good. Can one really argue against the legitimacy of their feelings? He had mercilessly tortured them. So why would they believe him? The situation did not look good, but once again, God gave Paul favor.

This time, He connected Paul with a man named Barnabas, who took him before the apostles and spoke on his behalf (Acts 9:27-30). As time progressed, these two men carried on the work of the ministry (Acts 11:25; 13:1-3). But after a dispute broke out between them, they parted ways (Acts 15:39). You have to realize that all relationships go through changes. Some will stand the test of time. Some will not. Just know that whatever happens, God has made provision for every twist and turn in your life.

Such was the case with Paul. When Barnabas faded off the scene, God allowed him to cross the path of a young man named Timothy (See Acts 16: 1-5). Paul took him under his wing, mentored him, and prepared him for the work of the ministry. As it turned out, Timothy played a vital role in Paul's mission. He assisted in evangelism, church planting, and converting many souls for Christ. Even when Paul was intensely persecuted and imprisoned, Timothy remained loyal and continued the work of the ministry. This goes to show you, God will build a circle of people around you to help you reach your place of destiny.

❧ BE TEACHABLE ❧

As God elevates you for His glory, never become too arrogant to be taught. You must never assume that you do not need Godly counsel from others who are more experienced and knowledgeable than you. "…In a multitude of counselors *there is* safety" (Proverbs 24:6b NKJV). As you grow and develop, recognize that you are occupying a dual role. In effect, you are both the student and the teacher. It has to be this way because whenever you cease to learn, you cease to grow.

How do you expect to aid in the development of others, if you aren't constantly improving? As you give out, let your spiritual leaders pour back into you. As you humble yourself, God will enlarge you. "Humble yourselves in the sight of the Lord, and He will lift you up" (James 4:10 NKJV). I was taught, "The way up is down."

I am not suggesting you submit to abusive, tyrannical authority. That is not God's will. I'm speaking of leaders that He has assigned to assist you along the way. You need to draw from the knowledge and experience of Godly fathers and mothers in the faith. Leave the Lone Ranger mentality behind. If you want to receive God's best, you must honor the anointing on the lives of those God has appointed to speak life into your spirit.

Adopt the posture of Mary, who dropped everything to sit at the feet of Jesus as he taught (Luke 10:38–41). Unlike her sister, Martha, who was busy preparing a feast for her guests, Mary seized the opportunity to receive an impartation of wisdom from the Master. Rather than worrying about natural hunger, she focused on the kind of hunger that could only be satisfied by the Bread of Life. Mary recognized that, "…man shall not live by bread alone; but man lives by every word that proceeds from the mouth of the LORD" (Deuteronomy 8:3c NKJV). She sat engrossed in the powerful teaching of Jesus, while Martha brooded.

"But Martha was distracted with much serving, and she approached Him and said, 'Lord, do you not care that my sister has left me to serve alone? Therefore tell her to help me.' And Jesus answered and said to her, 'Martha, Martha, you are worried and troubled about many things. But one thing is needed, and Mary has chosen that good part, which will not be taken away from her'" (Luke 10:40–42 NKJV).

Don't be like Martha. She wanted to serve, but she missed seizing the opportunity to connect to the one who could teach her. It is not enough to know how to work, if you don't have any Word. Swallow your pride and recognize, you can't get where you need to go in God without sound wisdom and instruction. Don't be zealous for a platform, without being equally zealous for the Word. Be disciplined enough to let someone else train you. If you do, the blessing that is on their life will flow to you.

This is what happened to Elisha when he stayed connected to the prophet Elijah, his mentor. In 1 Kings 19:18-21, Elijah was instructed by God to anoint Elisha as prophet. When the time came for Elisha to follow Elijah, he had to make a clean break from all that was familiar to him. It was not easy to do, but he still chose to seize the moment. "Then Elijah passed by him and threw his mantle on him. And he left the oxen and ran after Elijah and said, 'Please let me kiss my father and my mother, and then I will follow you'" (19:19b-20 NKJV). Are you willing to do whatever's necessary to fulfill your life's purpose? Are you prepared to submit and be trained? Are you willing to humbly serve others? Certainly Elisha was.

"But Jehoshaphat said, '*Is there* no prophet of the LORD here that we may inquire of the LORD by him?' So one of the servants of the king of Israel answered and said, 'Elisha the son of Shaphat *is* here, who poured water on the hands of Elijah'" (2 Kings 3:11 NKJV). I'm reminded of what the great Bible commentator, Matthew Henry, said, "He that will be great, let him learn to minister: he that will rise high, let him begin low." Always remember, greatness *is* service, and in order to lead effectively, you must learn to follow. Jesus said, "...but whoever desires to become great among you shall be your servant" (Mark 10:43b NKJV).

Elisha eagerly submitted to the mentorship of Elijah, just as Timothy did with Paul. Are you beginning to see a pattern here? There is no substitute for being teachable. It's necessary for your elevation. I would be misleading you, if I allowed you to think otherwise. Even in secular society, you cannot take on a new position without orientation. You have to be trained. The same is true in the Kingdom of God.

SOMETIMES THE KEY TO MOVING FORWARD, IS JUST BEING STILL.

Before God gives you a platform, he sets men and women over you to coach you. You have to get a little experience first, some on-the-job training. How else do you expect to be prepared? I want you to change your mind about submission. It is not a burden, it is a blessing. The enemy wants you to rebel because he knows that humility is the very thing that positions you for promotion. Being steadfast and faithful will take you where you need to go. Sometimes the key to moving forward, is just being still.

In 2 Kings 2:1–17, before Elijah ascends to heaven by a whirlwind, Elisha refuses to leave him. He stays by his side. Wherever Elijah went, Elisha followed. Each of the three times his master asked him to stay behind, he replied, "*As* the Lord lives, and *as* your soul lives I will not leave you!" (2:1b, 4b, 6b). Elisha was determined to receive an impartation from this mighty man of God. When the time of Elijah's departure drew near, he said to Elisha, "Ask! What may I do for you, before I am taken away from you?" (2 Kings 2:9a NKJV). By staying connected and humble, Elisha was properly aligned to receive what God had for him.

Elisha didn't hold back either as you can tell by his request. He said, "Please let a double portion of your spirit be upon me" (1 Kings 2:9b NKJV). Even Elijah admitted that what he asked was pretty lofty. He said, "You have asked a hard thing" (1 Kings 2:10a NKJV). You see, the blessing Elisha asked for was really reserved for the firstborn son (Deuteronomy 1:17). By law, he did not meet the eligibility requirements.

Ordinarily, that would have put him out of the running, but his loyalty compensated for what his credentials lacked. Elijah told him, "*Nevertheless,* if you see me *when I am* taken away from you, it shall be so for you; but if not, it shall not be so" (1 Kings 2:10b NKJV). The literal translation of the phrase, "if you see me" is, "if you see me eye to eye." Isn't that powerful? He assured Elisha that his request would be granted, if he could see what Elijah saw; in other words, if he could share his vision.

Sure enough, Elisha grabbed hold to what his master said and watched him ascend to heaven. What happened next? "Then he took the mantle of Elijah that had fallen from him, and struck the water, and said, 'Where is the LORD God of Elijah?' And when he also had struck the water, it was divided this way and that; and Elisha crossed over" (1 Kings 2:14 NKJV). The Lord honored him that day. He received a double portion of the anointing on Elijah's life, because he was teachable and faithful.

You can learn from this that God will send people to pour into your life who can help you be more productive. But you must have the spirit of Timothy, Mary, and Elisha. You have to be willing to sit down at someone else's feet and learn. You just stay humble and let God do the exalting. "For whoever exalts himself will be humbled, and he who humbles himself will be exalted" (Luke 14:11 NKJV). When is the last time you took a seat and received instruction from a seasoned spiritual leader? If you haven't lately, you need to. It will expedite your learning, growth, and development.

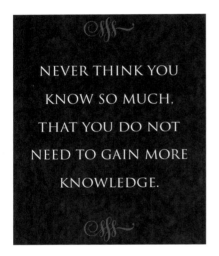

NEVER THINK YOU KNOW SO MUCH, THAT YOU DO NOT NEED TO GAIN MORE KNOWLEDGE.

Never think you know so much that you do not need to gain more knowledge. That is a trick of the enemy. Make a decision today to stay connected. It will be a great blessing to your life. Draw from the well of wisdom God has placed in front of you. When you do, you will achieve great feats for the Kingdom of God. Before we move on to the final chapter, I want to share a brief story with you.

At a meeting of top salespeople from around the country, the special guest speaker was a legendary salesman. Everyone in the organization considered him to be a brilliant man, because he consistently had the highest sales figures of any other salesman in his company for over 20 years. Through his acumen and hard work, he had even earned more money than the owner of his organization.

When he arose from his seat, everyone watched him walk to the front of the expansive room. He was a tall, lean man wearing an expensive tailor-made suit and a solid gold watch. He stood at the front of the room, smiled and said, "Good afternoon, gentlemen. You all know who I am. So, I'll get right to it. I am now going to reveal the secret of my success."

As you can probably imagine, when he said that, everyone's ears perked up and a wave of silence flooded the room. You could have heard a pin drop. Everyone just sat still in anxious expectation of the *secret*.

Then he said, "I wrote the secret down on a piece of paper and I put it right here in this envelope."

He held up a white envelope and everyone waited for him to open it. He then lowered the envelope and said, "But since I believe that success must be earned, I'm not going to *give* you the envelope. Instead, I'm going to *sell* the envelope to the highest bidder." Sensing a little tension in the room, he said, "Don't worry, you have my word that the envelope contains exactly what I said—the secret of my success, not only in sales, but in life."

The bidding started slowly at first...$5, then $10, then $50, $100, $130, $150, $200. Finally, one of his colleagues bought the envelope for $1,000. He did not open it until he got home that night. He couldn't wait to learn, "the secret of success." What do you think was written on the piece of paper? In my opinion, what was written on that piece of paper is worth much more than $1,000.

That night the winner of the auction eagerly tore open the envelope, unfolded the piece of paper, and read the following hand-written words: "The Secret to Success is Matthew 6:33."

Just remember this. Don't seek after folk. Seek after God. If you do that, He'll connect you to the right people.

CHAPTER 7

GET OUT OF THE BOAT

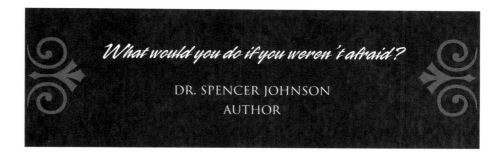

What would you do if you weren't afraid?

DR. SPENCER JOHNSON
AUTHOR

Embodied in this final chapter is the culmination of every lesson you have learned in this book. Now is the time for excuses to be eliminated and God's plan to be actuated. Finally, you have come to a crossroads where orientation has ended and implementation has begun. It's your season to *get out of the boat* and launch out into the deep. You are already equipped with everything you need to carry out God's will. Just as Jesus beckoned Peter, He is calling you at this very hour to boldly take steps of faith. In so doing, you will be headed toward the discovery of the full manifestation of His will for your life.

And when the disciples saw Him walking on the sea, they were troubled, saying, "It is a ghost!" And they cried out for fear. But immediately Jesus spoke to them, saying, "Be of good cheer! It is I; do not be afraid." And Peter answered Him and said, "Lord, if it is You, command me to come to You on the water." *So He said, "Come." And when Peter had come down out of the boat, he walked on the water to go to Jesus.* (Matthew 14:26-29 NKJV)

Did you observe that when Jesus summoned Peter he did not procrastinate? He didn't confer with the other disciples to see whether walking on water was a wise venture. On the contrary, as soon as he was sure the Master was beckoning him, he climbed out of that boat and started walking. He moved instantly. So what are you waiting for? Take your cues from Peter. If you have full assurance that God is calling you, get up and get moving. The ball is in your court. It's your call. This is your moment to take everything you know and put it into action.

God is not going to drag you kicking and screaming. Under no

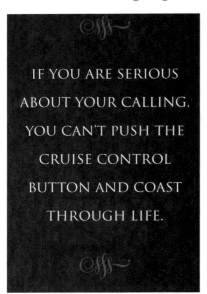

IF YOU ARE SERIOUS ABOUT YOUR CALLING, YOU CAN'T PUSH THE CRUISE CONTROL BUTTON AND COAST THROUGH LIFE.

circumstances will He make you launch out into the deep. He will only beckon. It's up to you to respond. You can think about it or you can be about it. Which will you choose? You can't afford to just sit back and do nothing. If you are serious about your calling, you can't push the cruise control button and coast through life. You have to be actively involved in what God is doing.

This is not Hollywood. There is no Santa Claus, Tooth Fairy, or Easter

Bunny coming to bring you goodies. Chances are the crew from Publisher's Clearing House Sweepstakes is not going to show up at your door with balloons, a microphone, a video camera, confetti, champagne, and a giant check for 10 million dollars. So, back away from the lottery ticket, and let go of the *"dollar and a dream"* mentality. You are going to have to get out of the boat and take action, in order to see the manifestation of your purpose.

The scripture found in James 2:26 brings this truth to the fore, "For as the body without the spirit is dead, so faith without works is dead also" (NKJV). To put it plainly, stop hoping for things to happen in your life without any effort on your part. You cannot circumvent the process of putting your faith to work. I can't speak for you, but I don't believe in just "naming it and claiming it." That's unhealthy, unbiblical, and unrealistic. There must be a balance between practical and spiritual things.

Don't be one of those who walk around with the "be warmed and filled" mindset. James 2:15–17 says, "If a brother or sister is naked and destitute of daily food, and one of you says to them, 'Depart in peace, be warmed and filled,' but you do not give them the things which are needed for the body, what *does it* profit? Thus also faith by itself, if it does not have works, is dead" (NKJV). James was drawing a comparison in this particular passage to make the point that faith is not one dimensional. It requires belief and action to be effective. The two work hand-in-hand.

That makes perfect sense, right? The same is true of your relationship with God. It's a collaborative effort, a partnership. You are working in tandem, in unison, in sync. God is not going to do everything and He's not asking you to do everything either. He does His part and you have to do yours. He works through you to accomplish His will, but He doesn't do things for you that you can do for yourself. He calls you, but you must abandon your safety net and come. You must use your gifts and abilities to bring your vision into existence. He has given you the power. He has given you the strength. Now you have to tap into it, and use it for His glory.

Proverbs 18:16 says, "A man's gift makes room for him, and brings him before great men" (NKJV). Yes, your gift does make room for you, but it's up to you to occupy the space. Consider the scripture in Deuteronomy 8:18, "And you shall remember the LORD your God, for *it is* He who gives you power to get wealth, that He may establish His covenant which He swore to your fathers, as *it is* this day" (NKJV).

Clearly, the scripture doesn't say God *gives you wealth*. It says He gives you the *power to get wealth*. God expects you to use the abilities and talents He's given you, as a means of obtaining the inheritance that is rightfully yours. If you want to see results in your life, you have to take some initiative. Work toward your goals. Begin doing something. If you want more, go after it.

Most assuredly, we need God. We can do nothing without Him. "For in Him we live and move and have our being" (Acts 17:28 NKJV). Anything we have is only because He has been gracious enough to bestow it upon us. God's goodness, however, does not negate the need for practicality. There's no way to avoid being responsible and accountable. Get busy doing the things that facilitate the manifestation of your dreams. I'm talking about realistic things:

- Save some money.
- Apply for a new job.
- Get a website.
- Purchase business cards.
- Create your business plan.
- Re-do your resume.
- Start exercising.
- Finish your manuscript.
- Pay down your debt.
- Market your business.
- Ask for a letter of recommendation.
- Go back to school.

These things are practical steps. That's your part. After you've done all you can, then you trust God to do what you cannot do. Stop waiting for Him to physically pull you out of your boat because that ain't gonna happen. Instead, you have to find the gumption to make that leap. Then you will see His extraordinary provision. Dig down deep and find the nerve to do something you've never done before.

DON'T BE A SPECTATOR, BE A PARTICIPATOR

It was a picturesque afternoon on the beach in Cancun, Mexico. As my wife and I relaxed in the sun with a couple of friends, we sat back and watched brave souls parasailing through the air. The more we observed, the more my curiosity increased. My friend and I began debating back and forth about whether we should try it. I made a deal with him. I said, "If you go, I'll go too." After mulling it over for a bit longer, I got up the courage to go for it.

I must admit. I had never participated in an activity quite as adventurous as this one. I felt a twinge of fear, but I beat it back and forged ahead anyway. I thought to myself, "C'mon Lawrence, how bad can this really be? People do this all the time. It'll be over before you know it." The more I psyched myself up, the better I felt.

Once we were safely strapped into the harness, I took a deep breath and we were on our way. The boat picked up speed pretty quickly. Within moments we were airborne. *Wow!* I thought, *This is really going to be…* But before I could finish my thought, our parachute was coming in for a crash landing. Boom! We smashed onto shore. Thankfully, neither of us was seriously hurt. I was pretty riled up, however, about losing my brand new shades. Come to find out, my friend and I were supposedly too heavy to ride together. (It would've been nice if someone had told us that before we came plummeting to earth.) How ironic. The one formerly known as "stick pencil," was now *too heavy*. Go figure!

You might expect that after such a traumatic experience, I would have been done with parasailing in perpetuity, right? Nope, not me…I was going back in, even though I had to go it alone. My mother didn't raise a quitter. Once again, I strapped up and settled in. I was feeling pretty relaxed at first. I had no idea how quickly my newfound confidence would wane.

As I lifted higher and higher above ground, my heart sank lower and lower. The people beneath me looked as small as ants. I kept thinking, *Am I supposed to be this high? What if I fall again? Will I make it out alive?* The next time I looked down, I saw at least ten sharks swimming in the water below. All I could hear was the theme music from the movie Jaws…"Duh-Nuh, Duh-Nuh, Duh-Nuh, Duh-Nuh, Duh-Nuh." I felt myself panicking. I did not want to be shark bait.

On average, the parachute is supposed to reach about 400 feet above ground. Surely, I must've been at about 800 feet…at least that's how I felt.

I careened above hotel rooftops. I could see down into the air conditioning units. I couldn't help thinking, *If I die after slamming into one of those things, I'm going to look terrible in my casket.* That was the last straw. I had no pride, no shame, and no composure. I was having a full blown meltdown. I called on Jesus like it was my last time. I prayed in English and in tongues. I said, "Please God, I promise, if you get me out of this alive, I will never, ever, ever do anything like this again!" Needless to say, I made it out alive.

What's the moral of the story? When you abandon your comfort zone you will no doubt be afraid. But don't let that stop you. Just go for it and you'll rise higher than you ever expected.

Do you want to be a spectator or a participator in life? You choose. Either step up to the plate, or step aside. Make a home run, or run home. Take a stand, or stand down. Stop vacillating. Make up your mind. Are you going after your purpose, or not? If not, you can always remain on the sidelines. Not to worry, you'll have more than enough company. There are plenty of passive participants that never get in the game. They watch from the stands, cheering, jeering, and judging; some silently, others rambunctiously. They live vicariously through the players on the field, who were brave enough to take a swing at life. Where do you want to be—in the bleachers or on the field?

Granted, the potential for failure and injury is a powerful deterrent for many people. But if you want more out of life, you have to be willing to take the good with the bad. Inevitably, storms will arise. There will be rainy days. It won't always be "smooth parasailing." Sometimes you'll come crashing to shore, but you'll be alright. Just as Peter did, you will occasionally stumble. He too, got momentarily tripped up by the ominous circumstances facing him. "But when he saw that the wind *was* boisterous, he was afraid; and beginning to sink he cried out, saying, 'Lord, save me!' And immediately Jesus stretched out *His* hand and caught him, and said to him, 'O you of little faith, why did you doubt?' And when they got into the boat, the wind ceased" (Matthew 14:30-32 NKJV).

When Peter looked down at the roaring seas beneath his feet and thought of the prospect of drowning, he lost his nerve. Similarly, when I looked down in the water while parasailing, I began thinking about all the things that could go wrong. As a result, I lost heart.

We all, from time to time, will get tripped up. That's a given. But we must be like Peter. He regained his composure, called on Jesus, grabbed His hand, and walked back to the boat. What an amazing display of resilience and fortitude on his part. That's why I find it interesting that, so many people condemn Peter for being afraid. From my vantage point, he is more worthy of commendation, than condemnation. After all, he was the only one of the disciples brave enough to leave his comfort zone. Though he temporarily lost his footing, at least he dared to do something.

This powerful excerpt taken from a speech given by Teddy Roosevelt at the Sorbonne in Paris, France on April 23, 1910, makes my point.

> It is not the critic who counts; not the man who points out how the strong man stumbles, or where the doer of deeds could have done them better. The credit belongs to the man who is actually in the arena, whose face is marred by dust and sweat and blood; who strives valiantly; who errs, who comes short again and again, because there is no effort without error and shortcoming; but who does actually strive to do the deeds; who knows great enthusiasms, the great devotions; who spends himself in a worthy cause; who at the best knows in the end the triumph of high achievement, and who at the worst, if he fails, at least fails while daring greatly, so that his place shall never be with those cold and timid souls who neither know victory nor defeat.

Wherever you are right now, I want you to pause and whisper a little prayer. Say, "Lord, please empower me take bold steps toward the fulfillment of my life's purpose. Help me to always trust Your faithfulness to perform Your word concerning me, in Jesus' name. Amen." (Read Hebrews 10:23.) Whenever you feel tempted to hide behind fear of failure, I want you to say that prayer. That way, you'll never be too afraid to "get in the arena" and strive to achieve your goals.

As you well know, you will sometimes face tough challenges, but you can remain grounded in the knowledge that whatever the obstacle, the Lord is on your side. The Master won't let you be swallowed up by the raging seas of life. When He sees you faltering, He will extend His hand and guide you to safety. Don't focus on your circumstances. Instead, look to Jesus. Call to mind what David said, "Yea, though I walk through the valley of the shadow of death, I will fear no evil; for You *are* with me; Your rod and Your staff, they comfort me" (Psalm 23:4 NKJV). Whenever you feel fear creeping in, remind yourself that you're not in this thing alone. No matter how intimidating or perilous your circumstances, God has got your back.

❦ MAKE YOUR MOVE ❦

There was a motivational trainer who was in demand all over the country. He was known for his ability to communicate profound truths utilizing simple parables and stories. No matter where he went, he began each workshop, seminar, and training, the exact same way. He addressed diverse audiences, but he posed the same question to each one. Here's what he would say:

"Once there were three frogs in the middle of the pond. They were each sitting on lily pads. One day, one of the frogs decided to jump into the pond. So how many frogs were left sitting on the lily pads?

"Well … What's your answer? Did you say two?

"Great! But wrong. The answer is actually three. You see, the one frog decided to jump into the pond, but he never actually did it. Deciding and jumping are not the same. Why? Deciding is a thought and jumping is an action."

If you're struggling with feelings of uncertainty about whether or not you should get out of the boat, I want to encourage you. Don't worry. Don't fear. God is giving you the nod. You're the one for the job, remember? You have the green light. Take your foot off the brake, put the pedal to the metal and go. Come on. Don't stall at the light. Don't freeze up. Get up. Make your move.

Let the impotent man at the pool of Bethesda serve as your model. The Bible records, "Now there is in Jerusalem by the Sheep Gate a pool, which is called in Hebrew, Bethesda, having five porches. In these lay a great multitude of sick people, blind, lame, paralyzed, waiting for the moving of the water. For an angel went down at a certain time into the pool and stirred up the water; then whoever stepped in first, after the stirring of the water, was made well of whatever disease he had" (John 5:2-4 NKJV).

Did you notice that the Scripture does not reveal the specific nature of this man's ailment? We are not sure whether he was lame, blind, or otherwise impaired. All we know for sure is that he had suffered with this infirmity for nearly four decades. He obviously had some mobility, because he had made previous attempts to get to the water, but things never quite worked out for him. Essentially, he had spent 38 long years feeling helpless, hapless, and hopeless. Yet, his life would change the day he came face to face with Jesus Christ.

"When Jesus saw him lying there, and knew that he already had been *in that condition* a long time, He said to him, 'Do you want to be made well?' The sick man answered Him, 'Sir, I have no man to put me into the pool when the water is stirred up; but while I am coming, another steps down before me'" (John 5:6-7 NKJV). By the time Jesus arrived on the scene, this man's frustration was palpable. He had put forth his best efforts to change his circumstance, to no avail. There always seemed to be someone a little faster and more agile than he. Surely, he must have thought he would die in the same miserable condition.

Little did he know, man's impossibility is God's opportunity. The help he sought for so long had finally come. It did not matter that he had been stuck for all those years. "Jesus said to him, 'Rise, take up your bed and walk.' And immediately the man was made well, took up his bed, and walked" (John 5:8 NKJV). When Jesus gave him the command, like Peter, he didn't hesitate. He didn't ask any questions. He just got up. He made a move. And in a single moment, his life changed forever.

There is something very significant I want to call to your attention. This impotent man received his healing instantaneously, but he did not know who Jesus was. It all started when the Jews got upset because this man was carrying his bed on the Sabbath; that was considered a violation of the Law of Moses (John 5:10). Consequently, they wanted to know who told him to carry his bed. Here's how the Bible records it, "Then they asked him, 'Who is the Man who said to you, 'Take up your bed and walk' But the one who was healed did not know who it was, for Jesus had withdrawn, a multitude being in that place" (John 5:12-13 NKJV).

Did you see that? It wasn't until later, in the temple, that he discovered the identity of the One who had healed him (John 5:14, 15).

You have to be hungry for your change, so when opportunity knocks, you'll respond in kind. The impotent man desperately wanted deliverance. He made a move at the command of a stranger. He threw caution to the wind and took Jesus at His Word. He did not even have the luxury of knowing that he was in the presence of God incarnate. He did not realize that the Living Word had just spoken a word to him. All he knew is he wanted to be made whole.

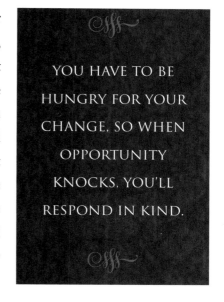

YOU HAVE TO BE HUNGRY FOR YOUR CHANGE, SO WHEN OPPORTUNITY KNOCKS, YOU'LL RESPOND IN KIND.

You know who God is. You are fully aware of His Deity and power. Why then, should you be afraid to make a move? Don't you realize the same Jesus Who delivered the impotent man is alive in you right now? He is ready to show Himself strong on your behalf. All you need to do is heed His call. The moment you make your move, He will make His. As the saying goes, "If you take one step, He'll take two."

He will meet you at your point of need, but you must follow hard after Him. You have got to be willing to do what blind Bartimaeus did when he discovered that Jesus was close by.

The Biblical account reads, "And when he heard that it was Jesus of Nazareth, he began to cry out and say, 'Jesus, Son of David, have mercy on me!' Then many warned him to be quiet; but he cried out all the more, 'Son of David, have mercy on me!'" (Mark 10:47-48 NKJV). From the very beginning we see that Bartimaeus wasn't willing to allow this opportunity to pass him by. He did not care what people said, or what they thought. Nothing else mattered in that moment, except getting to Jesus. When people shushed him, he got louder. When they tried to calm him, he grew more boisterous. His breakthrough was on the line and he was determined to get it.

Bartimaeus' resoluteness paid off. "So Jesus stood still and commanded him to be called. Then they called the blind man, saying to him, 'Be of good cheer. Rise, He is calling you'" (Mark 10:49 NKJV). Notice how the reaction of the people shifted once they got wind of the fact that Jesus was calling for Bartimaeus. Those who had been telling him to shut up were now saying hurry up. They stopped criticizing him and started motivating him. They quit restraining him and started rooting him on.

Many times, you will have to make your move despite the disapproval of people. They'll tell you how crazy it is, until it starts working. They'll say it can't be done, until you succeed at it. Then the very ones who spoke against you will speak in favor of you. Don't be sidetracked by the scathing remarks of others. Press forward anyway. Drown out those negative voices and make your move.

It's going to work. You will be prosperous. God will exalt you right in the midst of those who talked about you. Do not worry about them. They will jump on the bandwagon later. In the meantime, just keep doing what you're doing. It will all pay off in the end. You might be seen as a deviant now, but just remember, today's rebel is tomorrow's pioneer. People might be mocking you, but they won't get the last laugh. As long as you have the attention of the One with the power to change your circumstance, that is all that matters.

Being persistent certainly paid off for Bartimaeus and the same will happen for you. "So Jesus answered and said to him, 'What do you want Me to do for you?' The blind man said to Him, 'Rabboni, that I may receive my sight.' Then Jesus said to him, 'Go your way; your faith has made you well.' And immediately he received his sight and followed Jesus on the road" (Mark 10:51-52 NKJV). That day, he received more than his sight; he got a brand new lease on life.

Through Bartimaeus' story, we see that with persistence, anything is possible. He was just a blind beggar who refused to give up. Is the same true of you? Are you willing to vigorously pursue what God has for you? Make up your mind to chase after His will. Run after your destiny and when you do, you'll ultimately come away with the prize. Even when Bartimaeus was blind, he had enough foresight to be unrelenting in his pursuit of healing. "Do you not know that those who run in a race all run, but one receives the prize? Run in such a way that you may obtain *it*. And everyone who competes *for the prize* is temperate in all things. Now they *do it* to obtain a perishable crown, but we *for* an imperishable *crown*" (1 Corinthians 9:24, 25 NKJV).

There is a powerful excerpt I want to share with you from motivational speaker, Les Brown's, book, *Live your Dreams*.

I have a little affirmation, written by author Berton Braley, that I say at times when I need to build up my courage and to focus on my dreams and goals. Say this when you need to do the same.

"If you want a thing bad enough to go out and fight for it, to work day and night for it, to give up your time, your peace and your sleep for it…if all that you dream and scheme is about it, and life seems useless and worthless without it…if you gladly sweat for it and fret for it and plan for it and lose all your terror of the opposition for it…if you simply go after that thing you want with all of your capacity, strength and sagacity, faith, hope and confidence and stern pertinacity…if neither cold, poverty, famine, nor gout, sickness nor pain, of body and brain, can keep you away from the thing that you want…if dogged and grim you beseech and beset it, with the help of God, you WILL get it!" (New York: Avon Books, 1992, p. 130)

How badly do you want it? If you know in your heart that life is meaningless without your purpose, then stop at nothing to attain it. It takes great strength and determination, but with the help of the Lord, you'll reach higher heights than you ever thought imaginable. As I stated earlier, the most important thing is taking God at His word. Even in the times when situations seem unlikely to work out, still trust Him. With God, all things are possible.

Do you believe that firmly enough to get out of the boat? There is a fundamental difference between knowing God is able to do the impossible and believing He will do it for you. Not only is He the God of Abraham, Isaac, and Jacob; He is also your God (Matthew 22:32). He wants to bless you and pour out His goodness upon you. But before you can ever step out in faith and receive His abundant favor, you have to condition your mind.

Get to a place where you eagerly anticipate a supernatural influx of blessings. Jesus said, "I have come that they may have life, and that they may have it more abundantly" (John 10:10 NKJV). The word "life" in this Scripture, comes from the Greek word "zoe," which basically means "The God kind of life." And the word "abundant" in this same passage, is derived from the Greek word "perissos," which means "superabundant and ever-flowing." With this in mind, you can be confident about the outcome of your future. As long as you remain in His will, bountiful blessings and miracles will flow to you.

Furthermore, Jesus assures us that, "If you abide in Me, and My words abide in you, you will ask what you desire, and it shall be done for you" (John 15:7 NKJV). He has an endless supply of whatever you need. The question is do you believe you can have it? This is the key to your release.

I want to share a story that will serve as a reminder of what can happen when you don't trust God enough to make a move. As you walk along your path to purpose, don't be like the Israelites whose limited perception of themselves robbed them of their promise.

According to Numbers chapters 33-36, God gave Israel both the approval and the instructions they needed to possess the land of Canaan. He left no stone unturned. Yet, when they got inside, they were intimidated by the opposition and didn't believe they were capable of conquering the giants. "There we saw the giants (the descendants of Anak came from the giants); and we were like grasshoppers in our own sight, and so we were in their sight" (Numbers 13:33 NKJV).

How unfortunate for Israel. After all the reassurance they had received from the Lord, they were unable to enlarge their thinking. Because of their small mentality, they cut themselves off from their inheritance and ended up dying in the wilderness. But the generation after them would possess the land of promise. "Moreover your little ones and your children, who you say will be victims, who today have no knowledge of good and evil, they shall go in there; to them I will give it, and they shall possess it. But as for you, turn and take your journey into the wilderness by the Way of the Red Sea" (Deuteronomy 1:39–40 NKJV).

Tragically, this particular generation of God's chosen people missed their moment. Worse yet, there was no second chance for them. You, on the other hand, still have an opportunity. The question then becomes, are you mentally prepared for it? How do you perceive yourself? I'm not talking about how you act publicly. I want you to focus on the thoughts you have privately; those are the ones that matter most.

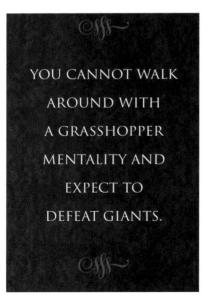

YOU CANNOT WALK AROUND WITH A GRASSHOPPER MENTALITY AND EXPECT TO DEFEAT GIANTS.

You cannot walk around with a grasshopper mentality and expect to defeat giants. You cannot be too afraid to make a move and still expect a breakthrough. From this point onward, see yourself as God sees you. Begin envisioning yourself inhabiting your place of promise.

When God speaks a word over your life you must visualize it and internalize it, so He can actualize it. The acronym for this principle is "V.I.A," just like the word *via,* which means "by way of," or "by means of." Essentially, I want you to recognize that reaching your God-given destiny is accomplished *via* visualization, internalization and actualization.

- **Visualize**—You've got to be able to see the unseen. Get a picture of it in your mind.
- **Internalize**—Embed it in your psyche, so it becomes a part of you.
- **Actualize**—Trust God to make it a reality in your life.

Get it down in your spirit. Rehearse it in your mind. Believe it in your heart. And whatever you do, don't allow Satan to make you doubt it. He wants you to question God's plan and purpose concerning you, so he can rob you of your tenacity and resolve. If you don't believe that something is possible, you will not even pursue it. You will not make a move. You will lose your focus. You will become lethargic. You will give up on it. David says it this way, "*I would have lost heart,* unless I had believed that I would see the goodness of the LORD in the land of the living" (Psalm 27:13 NKJV). You must resist the temptation to doubt. Tell yourself, "My heart is fixed and my mind is made up. If God said it, I believe it and that settles it." Then, act on what you know.

❦ TRUST GOD'S FAITHFULNESS ❦

Be unflinching in your expectation, knowing that God is faithful. As long as you focus on His faithfulness, you can remain steadfast despite your situation. "By faith Sarah herself also received strength to conceive seed, and she bore a child when she was past the age, because she judged Him faithful who had promised" (Hebrews 11:11 NKJV). There was absolutely no way that she, in her physical condition, could have successfully delivered a baby. Unquestionably, she needed a miracle. Outwardly, it appeared her time had come and gone. By human criteria, she was too old, too feeble, and too late. But with God, all things are possible.

Even when your circumstances don't line up with His word, never forget that He is sovereign. He is God all by Himself. "I *am* the LORD, and *there* is no other; *There* is no God besides Me" (Isaiah 45:5 NKJV). He is infinite in wisdom and limitless in power. God is the Supreme Ruler and all things are subject to His authority. There is nothing in heaven or earth that falls outside His domain. "The earth is the LORD's, and all its fullness, the world and those who dwell therein" (Psalm 24:1 NKJV). Understand that it does not matter what it looks like, God is always in control.

That is what Sarah had to realize before she could see God move in her life. Certainly the prospect of having a child didn't look promising for her. Early on, she had so desperately wanted to conceive, but God had not seen fit to open her womb. In Genesis 15:4, the Lord promised her husband Abraham that he would produce an heir. "…the word of the Lord *came* to him, saying '…one who will come from your own body shall be your heir'" (NKJV). Quite naturally, Sarah must have assumed that she would conceive soon after, but that did not happen. Years passed and she was still barren. She must have been wondering, "Why can't I have children? Has God forgotten about me? Am I not part of His Divine plan?"

She spent ten years waiting, to no avail. Finally, in her desperation, she introduced a surrogate to compensate for her barrenness. "And she had an Egyptian maidservant whose name was Hagar. So Sarai said to Abram, 'See now, the LORD has restrained me from bearing *children*. Please, go in to my maid; perhaps I shall obtain children by her'" (Genesis 16:1-2 NKJV). Thus, Hagar conceived.

This, however, was not God's plan. As a matter of fact, the arrangement turned ugly before long. Once Hagar conceived, she began to despise Sarah. More than likely, she felt superior because she was the one carrying Abraham's baby, rather than his wife (Genesis 16:3–4). As a result of the jealous rivalry, Sarah was thoroughly frustrated, humiliated, and angry. At the height of her vexation, she went on a rampage, lashing out at Abraham and Hagar. She dealt so harshly with her handmaiden that she ran off into the wilderness (Genesis 16:5–6).

Do you see how Sarah's impetuous plan went awry? What she didn't realize is that God didn't need her help devising a strategy. He already knew what He was going to do. She had stopped trusting and started scheming. How many times have you done that? It usually doesn't turn out well, does it? Initially, it may seem to be going smoothly. Then, slowly but surely, things unravel. Before you know it, the situation has spiraled out of control and you are left with a mess.

Thankfully, God is merciful enough to intervene, even when we cause problems for ourselves. In this case, He sent an angel to Hagar to help patch things up. She was instructed to return back to the house of her Mistress and submit (Genesis 16:6-12). Hagar obeyed and later gave birth to Abraham's son, Ishmael. Although he was undeniably Abraham's seed, he was not the child of promise. On the contrary, he was the son of the flesh (Galatians 4:21-31). Not until fifteen years later would the full manifestation of God's Word be revealed. Unbeknownst to Sarah, she would give birth to her husband's heir.

After years of disappointment, she had probably completely dismissed the idea of ever conceiving. That is until she was eavesdropping on a conversation between Abraham and three out-of-town guests one day. One of the men was prophesying regarding Sarah. "And He said, 'I will certainly return to you according to the time of life, and behold, Sarah your wife shall have a son.' (Sarah was listening in the tent door which *was* behind him)" (Genesis 18:10 NKJV). When she first heard the news, she let out one big guffaw. The whole thing seemed so far fetched. "Therefore Sarah laughed within herself, saying, 'After I have grown old, shall I have pleasure, my lord being old also?'" (Genesis 18:12 NKJV).

Admittedly, a ninety-year old mom and a hundred-year old dad was an implausible idea. Yet, implausibility does not forego possibility. Just as God promised, Sarah conceived and bore Isaac, whose name meant, "laughter." "And Sarah said, 'God has made me laugh, and all who hear will laugh with me... Who would have said to Abraham that Sarah would nurse children? For I have borne *him* a son in his old age'" (Genesis 21:6-7 NKJV).

Everything came full circle, just as God intended from the beginning. You can be sure He will also work in your situation. You are going to give birth to your promise. It does not matter if you have been barren a long time. God is supernaturally opening your womb. You will be fruitful. You will be successful. You will be victorious. Even though you don't know how or when it's coming to pass, just believe it. Whatever you need, He will supply. Whatever you lack, He will supplement. I've seen Him do it time and again.

I vividly recall a dream I had some years ago. In it, I saw myself writing a check. The funds were not for me however, they were for a friend from college. The most poignant detail about the dream was that God showed me the exact dollar amount.

When I woke up, the Lord immediately spoke to my heart. He wanted to use me to be a blessing to my old acquaintance. With no hesitation, I got to work. But, I had one major hurdle to overcome; I didn't know where he was. How could I possibly wire money, without knowing where to send it?

The information I did have was very general. I knew he and his wife were overseas on the mission field, but I didn't have an exact location. I enlisted the help of my administrative team. Even with their assistance, however, searching for two missionaries in an obscure location was no easy feat. Surely, Satan tried to discourage me. He wanted me to doubt whether God had really told me to do it, but I refused to quit. We continued our search, until finally, we found the location. Immediately, I sent my administrative assistant to wire the money. I felt good knowing I had obeyed God. Then it hit me. I had not accounted for the service fees.

And you know what that meant. The figure I saw in my dream would not be the amount he received. I *had* to include the extra money, which is precisely what I did.

What a sense of relief I felt. Mind you, I still did not know why he needed the money, what he needed it for, or exactly when he had to have it. I was certain of nothing except the Lord told me to send it. For me, that was enough.

The answers, however, did eventually come. One day, he contacted me to say the financial seed came at a critical point in his ministry. He knew without a doubt, God had orchestrated the whole thing. As it turns out, he and his wife were right in the middle of an expansion effort and they were in dire need of more resources. Remarkably, not only was the timing right, but the amount was exactly what they needed to help carry on the vision.

That moment really impacted me. It taught me that God has limitless ways to bless us. You can always trust His faithfulness to come through for you. He is never out of options. He will do whatever it takes to make sure you are completely taken care of. He will supernaturally supply your needs. "And my God shall supply all your need according to His riches in glory by Christ Jesus" (Philippians 4:19 NKJV). From this moment on, I want you to start expecting a miracle. Stop looking at your deficiency and focus on His sufficiency. He will provide all that is necessary to fulfill your life's purpose.

He is "Jehovah-Jireh," which means, "The Lord will provide." This statement is derived from a pivotal moment in Abraham's life. God challenged him to offer up his promised child, Isaac, as a burnt offering (Genesis 22). Clearly, the nature of the Divine charge was extremely difficult. Still, at no time did Abraham refuse, rebut, or rebel. Rather, he remained calm, composed, and confident the entire time. He had seen the hand of God move on many occasions. He knew the Lord would not let him down.

I wonder, however, who in the story most truly depicts what your behavior would be, given the same scenario. Would you be like Abraham and demonstrate a mature faith? Or, would your response more closely resemble that of the immature Isaac? When he and his father were on their way up to the mountain he said, "Look, the fire and the wood, but where is the lamb for a burnt offering?" (Genesis 22:7 NKJV). Abraham responded, "My son, God will provide for Himself the lamb for a burnt offering" (Genesis 22:8 NKJV).

Granted, Isaac was very young and did not understand what was going on. Nevertheless, I want to juxtapose their responses in order to make a point. We learn from Abraham, the *Father of Faith*, how to live in expectation of the miraculous. On the other hand, we gather from Isaac how to operate from a position of logic. Where do you fit? When you are confronted with illogical circumstances, do you typically resort to tactical solutions or do you choose to trust God?

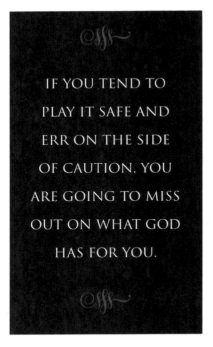

IF YOU TEND TO PLAY IT SAFE AND ERR ON THE SIDE OF CAUTION, YOU ARE GOING TO MISS OUT ON WHAT GOD HAS FOR YOU.

If you tend to play it safe and err on the side of caution, you are going to miss out on what God has for you. Abraham was only being tested. His faith was being proved. At no time did God intend to take the life of young Isaac. Instead, He was exemplifying His faithfulness to Abraham. But if Abraham had not endured intense testing, he could never have explored deeper levels of his faith in God. Have you ever noticed the more you *need* to trust Him, the more you *learn* to trust Him?

It's not until you are in the middle of a crisis situation, that you come to know His great delivering power. It isn't until He brings you through a serious dilemma, that you recognize, He's a present help in time of trouble (Psalm 46:1 NKJV). It's not until you do not know how to make ends meet that you learn, He will provide for every need. You may have heard some people say it this way: "If I never had a problem, how would I know He could solve it? If I never was sick, how would I know He could heal me?"

Each time you are faced with a different challenge, His grace, mercy, and faithfulness is revealed to you in a new way. "*Through the LORD's mercies we are not consumed, Because His compassions fail not. They are new every morning; Great is Your faithfulness*" (Lamentations 3:22-23 NKJV). It all comes down to knowing that you have a loving Father, Who only wants the best for you. Therefore, as you grow in your dependence upon Him, you will come to know Him as your Jehovah-jireh. Trust God's faithfulness. He will never let you down.

❧ DESPISE NOT THE DAY OF ❧ SMALL BEGINNINGS

What's your dream? What's your vision for your life? What has God called you to do? Are you stuck wondering how to make it happen? Do you wish God would just show you all the details? Once you identify your purpose, then you are left with the question of how. Please know, God's not going to show you everything. The blanks get filled in as you go along. You have to do the same thing we all must do. Get out of the boat. Start somewhere, anywhere. I started the church I pastor in a garage.

That's right, Agape Family Worship Center began on May 27, 1990, in my parents' garage. The congregation comprised a whopping seven adults and four children. We even had a name for our first location; we called it "God's Garage (G.G's)." We completely furnished it with a podium, carpeting, banners, and chairs. Last, but not least, we hung an elegant curtain to hide the tools. I'll admit it wasn't much, but I made a conscious decision to trust God, rather than focus on what I didn't have.

But, what if I didn't? What if I would have had too much pride to start a ministry in a garage? What if I decided to wait until I had more answers, more capital, and more connections? I had many opportunities to turn back. And sometimes, quite honestly, I wanted to give up. But the voice of the Holy Spirit kept speaking to me in dreams, in visions, and through others. He kept telling me to push forward.

If I had not obeyed the voice of God, where would I be today? I would be missing out on the satisfaction of feeding hungry children, ministering to individuals who are incarcerated, influencing souls through outreach, and going into countless of homes weekly through television and streaming media. Furthermore, I would not have seen our congregation grow from just eleven people to thousands of weekly attendants. It's truly overwhelming to stand back and look at what God has done.

Years ago, I wasn't certain about anything really. I had so many unanswered questions. I wondered: "How will people find out about the ministry? Will they be willing to worship in a garage? If so, will they want to join the church? Will I be a good pastor?" There was so much I didn't know. But it wasn't until I began putting one foot in front of the other that I learned the answers. As I walked it out, God worked it out.

YOUR STEPS MAY NOT BE ORGANIZED, BUT THEY ARE ORDERED.

Your steps may not be organized, but they are ordered. The sooner you understand that, the better off you'll be. No amount of strategic planning is going to change the fact that you won't have all the details. You can even draw up a five-year-plan if you want, but only God knows the end from the beginning. I'm not averse to organizing and strategizing. I just believe only God knows exactly where you're going and how you'll get there. It does not make sense to get bogged down trying to figure out all the steps in advance. You will only frustrate yourself.

There is no way of knowing everything. Just as I did, you may have to start small, but don't be embarrassed by humble beginnings. "For who has despised the day of small things?" (Zechariah 4:10a NKJV). As you trust the Lord, you will blossom into a mighty ambassador for His Kingdom. Just continue to keep the Word He has spoken over you in the forefront of your mind. Let it drive you. Let it fuel your passion. Let it carry you to the other side.

Jesus said to the disciples, "Let us go over to the other side." The fact that Jesus, Who is the Living Word, spoke a word, they were guaranteed to make it to their destination in one piece. But the disciples missed it, just as you and I do time and again. They heard what Jesus said, but they did not understand it.

Somehow, in the midst of their situation the disciples forgot the power of Jesus' Words. His Words are spirit and life, living and powerful (John 6:63; Hebrews 4:12). His Word *is* His guarantee (Isaiah 55:11). There is no need to worry about anything. God is absolutely going to bless you. Just get up and get going. It's time to fulfill your life's purpose. You have the tools. You have the favor. You have the power. He has the plan. Follow Him and watch the Lord turn your small beginning into a big breakthrough!

"'For I know the plans that I have for you,' declares the LORD, 'plans to prosper you and not to harm you, plans to give you hope and a future'" (Jeremiah 29:11 NIV). He has already equipped you with all you need to go forth and walk in your calling. Now it's up to you to get out of the boat. What are you going to do? It's your call.

ABOUT THE AUTHOR

Lawrence Raphael Powell is the Senior Pastor of Agape Family Worship Center in Rahway, New Jersey. With over eighteen years in ministry, Pastor Lawrence is transforming lives with his powerful, prolific and practical presentation of the Gospel. Thousands of families from across the tri-state region flock to Agape every week to experience warm fellowship, dynamic worship and anointed teaching. Through outreach, evangelism and multimedia broadcasting, Pastor Lawrence is bringing the Good News of Jesus Christ to people all over the world.

His beginnings were humble when he first answered the call of God to pastor in 1990. The first service was held in his parent's garage in Rahway. Only he and his wife Vanessa, along with 9 others, were in attendance. From a small garage, to the now state-of-the-art facility, known as *Agape Pointe,* Pastor Lawrence's mission still remains the same; "to proclaim and demonstrate the love of God to the world." His humble spirit and genuine heart for people endear him to diverse audiences of every ethnicity.

With a strong commitment and genuine passion for outreach and evangelism, under the leadership of Pastor Lawrence, Agape provides assistance to the local community and those in prison, by supplying much needed resources, materials and support services. Countless testimonies of hope, healing and transformation pour in, from those being touched and liberated through Agape's outreach efforts.

A much sought-after speaker, respected Biblical teacher, and author, Lawrence Powell earned a Bachelor's degree from Rutgers University and a Master's degree from Oral Roberts University. It is obvious to all who know him that he is preparing and positioning a mighty generation of leaders at Agape. It is a generation of world changers, poised to advance and expand the Kingdom for the glory of God. Lawrence and his wife, Vanessa, are the proud parents of three children, and reside in New Jersey.